If I Hold My Peace

If I Hold My Peace

By
Vivian Jones

XULON PRESS

Xulon Press
2301 Lucien Way #415
Maitland, FL 32751
407.339.4217
www.xulonpress.com

Unless otherwise indicated, Scripture quotations taken from the King James
Version (KJV) – *public domain*.

Printed in the United States of America.

ISBN-13: 978-1-54566-008-9

Dedication

This book is dedicated to the memory and history of my family-my ancestors – those who have gone on, long before I was born. It is also dedicated to those family members whose lives I have shared and have gleaned so much from. Being the seventh of my siblings has been a journey.

This book is dedicated to those who want to see their journey through life in print. It is possible. Do not fear. Do not worry about the way. Once your mind is made up the way will be made. If you feel that you have a burden or love for the next generation and would like to say so, you must think of those who will come after you. We all have something to say – your words, your journey, and your faith can always affect future generations. Future generations need a blueprint for the future.

This book is dedicated to each family member. It is our story of how we made it, how we lived our lives, how we persevered, how we used our faith and relationships with our God to navigate over hurdles and challenges, how we survived with such faith and dignity, how we stood the test of time, raising our families, facing disappointments, loving, marrying, burying our loved ones, and raising new generations. All that our lives touched, every prayer, every act of generosity, every moment spent on this earth – my prayer is that a life was touched, a life was healed, a dream became a reality.

This book is also dedicated to my little companion of almost 18 years, Christian, my precious little Shih Tzu, who passed on in October 2018. Christian is truly missed and loved.

Thank God for our foreparents, our loved ones who are still with us, and blessings upon those who will come after us!

-Amen-

Special Acknowledgements

Special thanks to my siblings: Wallace Johnson, Darlean Curry, Doris Duncan, Myrtle Collins, Manuel Leroy Carroll, Vernette Morning Star Carroll Kittrell, Ellis Carroll, Nadine Carroll Hayes, and Alfred Carroll.

Much appreciation to Sandra Fleming, typist and coordinator.

Table of Contents

Foreword

The focus of this book is on a Black American Family, whose challengers, struggles and successes are masterfully brought together through scholarly research into historical records and carefully review of oral history provided by the elders and others who knew the family.

Compiling this family history took the writer on a journey back to the mid 1800 during the life of Martha Williams Rainey, the mother of Florence Rainey, The family started on its journey soon after slavery full of hope for a better future, Believing that hard work and their faith in God would sustain them during this period of great uncertainty for black families. From generation to generation the family picking up momentum on this journey that brought it through a period of sharecropping, providing seasonal labor as hired field hands, and participating in the great migration north.

As one follows the history of this family, as told by Vivian Jones, it becomes clear to the reader that there been, and continues to be a strong matriarchal influence that has served as the glue that held the family together. She listened to stories about the many struggles to obtain formal training in all levels of education, about the hardships experienced in the work place,(which was the plantation fields), about involvement in campaigns for the right to participate in our democratic process, about work to remove old and new barriers of segregation and discrimination that would impede this family's progress; in fact the progress of all families.

Today this family is represented in most if not all areas of this society: Religion, business, law and justice, health care, military, entertainment, finance, science and engineering, technology and other major functional areas in both public and private sectors of this country.

We hope that this book will inspire other families to share and tell their stories.

Wallace L. Johnson

Introduction

I recall the exact moment I saw it. Researching my family history, searching for them in historical archives, I remember finally locating and seeing their names and realizing that my grandmother Florence was only five years of age at the time. I could only weep. I was finally able to look upon their names. This was the first documentation I had found showing my great-grandmother and great-grandfather, Cornelius and Martha Rainey, parents of my grandmother, Florence, had actually lived. Previously I could not find their names even in family Bibles. Now I was looking at their names on the United States Census! I truly had a moment of thanksgiving and connection engulfing me!

I truly believe I was assigned the work of this project to document history to tell who our foreparents were. I began to imagine what their lives must have been like, raising 15 children in the early 1800's, being sharecroppers a few years out of slavery and still not having real freedom, not being valued or respected by those whom you continued to labor for, or the society in which you lived. I continued to weep. Their lives must have been quite a challenge. Ironically, one hundred years later their descendants would face some of the same hurdles, challenges and injustices. Tears were very much in order.

The times that we are living in right now are very troubling. However, as people of color, we have an obligation to our ancestors to make every effort to uplift our race. We are to strive to leave seeds of hope for those who will come after us - our children who will inherit this world that we are leaving behind. Our children deserve to inherit seeds of hope and freedom for themselves and their posterity. We cannot rape the planet out of greed and man's inhumanity to his fellowman, and leave our children a legacy of woes and a planet that has almost been destroyed. Without the intervention of our Creator, it is a possibility that our seed will not inherit a sound world.

We cannot in good faith forget the struggles of our ancestors. They *never* realized the freedoms that we take for granted today. They could not dream of a day of freedom, not knowing what it truly felt like. They lived a life under racism and Jim Crow that we cannot imagine. We must not forget their struggles, their pain and how they survived. We are their seed. We must daily lift our brothers and sisters up. We must not allow others to tell us to forget the past. We must remember from whence we came and build on it for a better tomorrow. We must rewrite our own history, and not expect others to tell our story. Our story is unique, spiritual, and biblical. We are commanded to know who we are and from whence we came. If we do not learn from history and understand history, we forfeit our future. The universe challenges us to prepare for tomorrow. Jeremiah 6:16 states: *Thus saith the LORD, STAND YE IN THE WAYS, AND SEE, AND ASK FOR THE OLD PATHS, WHERE IS THE GOOD WAY, AND WALK THEREIN, AND YE SHALL FIND REST FOR YOUR SOULS.* We must look for our God to guide us, to open our eyes and ears to His leading.

We, as people of African descent and indigenous people of the Americas, have suffered enough. We have suffered from within and without. We must correct the challenges that we have created for ourselves. We must grow and evolve out of the situation that we find ourselves in today, not only in America, but around the globe. We must refuse to pass this same legacy on to succeeding generations.

There must be some closure to our struggle and our status here in America.

I pray that my children and grandchildren's generation will receive the torch that has been handed to them to forge ahead. I pray they will take the positive and the spiritual and lift our race to the level that the Creator intended. I pray that I have left them a legacy they can be proud of - a legacy attempting to learn from the past in order to leave the succeeding generation a better world.

⊰|ancestry

1880 United States Federal Census

Name:	Martha Rainey
Age:	26
Birth Year:	abt 1854
Birthplace:	Arkansas
Home in 1880:	Auburn, Lincoln, Arkansas
Race:	Mulatto
Gender:	Female
Relation to Head of House:	Wife
Marital Status:	Married
Spouse's Name:	Cornelius Rainey
Father's Birthplace:	Arkansas
Mother's Birthplace:	Arkansas
Occupation:	Laborer

Household Members:	Name	Age
	Cornelius Rainey	35
	Martha Rainey	26
	Emma Rainey	9
	Sampson Rainey	7
	Florence Rainey	5

Source Citation: Year: *1880*; Census Place: *Auburn, Lincoln, Arkansas*; Roll: *49*; Family History Film: *1254049*; Page: *16A*; Enumeration District: *174*; Image: *0579*

Source Information:

Ancestry.com and The Church of Jesus Christ of Latter-day Saints. *1880 United States Federal Census* [database on-line]. Provo, UT, USA: Ancestry.com Operations Inc, 2010. 1880 U.S. Census Index provided by The Church of Jesus Christ of Latter-day Saints © Copyright 1999 Intellectual Reserve, Inc. All rights reserved. All use is subject to the limited use license and other terms and conditions applicable to this site.

Original Data: Tenth Census of the United States, 1880. (NARA microfilm publication T9, 1,454 rolls). Records of the Bureau of the Census, Record Group 29. National Archives, Washington, D.C.

Description:
This database is an index to 50 million individuals enumerated in the 1880 United States Federal Census. Census takers recorded many details including each person's name, address, occupation, relationship to the head of household, race, sex, age at last birthday, marital status, place of birth, parents' place of birth. Additionally, the names of those listed on the population schedule are linked to actual images of the 1880 Federal Census.

© 2015 Ancestry

NOW

Chapter 1

"The Legacy"

"If we have forgotten the name of our God, or stretched out our hands to a strange god; shall not God search this out?
For He knoweth the secrets of the heart."

Psalm 44:20-21

According to the 1880 United States Federal Census, my great-grandmother, Martha, was married to Cornelius Rainey, my great grandfather, in Auburn, Lincoln County, Arkansas. Martha was 26 years of age and Cornelius was 35 years of age. One hundred and thirty-five years later - November 2015 – as thoughts of writing this book began to form in my mind, I'm sitting here thinking of my great-grandparents.

Martha Rainey, my great grandmother, was born in 1854 in Tennessee. Great-grandfather Cornelius was born in 1845 in Virginia. They were married in 1871. My great grandparents had 15 children, all of whom did not live.

According to the 1880 United States Federal census, Martha and Cornelius Rainey, had three children living in the home: Emma Rainey (9 years), Sampson (7 years) and Florence (5 years) – Florence, my grandmother.

Children listed in the 1900 Census were Jim Rainey (20 years), Henry Rainey (14 years), Lally Rainey (11 years), Roger Rainey (8 years), Langston Rainey (5 years) and Pearly Rainey (2 years).

We know very little about my great-grandparents. We were told they were devoted, God-fearing people. Martha and Cornelius Rainey lived a normal life within their surroundings. They were sharecroppers who, following

circumstances not of their own making but because of the times they were born into. They worked the land in order to have a place to live. According to oral history, which was passed on to us, my great grandparents would not realize owning their own home.

My grandmother Florence, who herself was charming and beautiful, often expressed that her mother (my great grandmother Martha) was most beautiful. She described her parents as being of Cherokee lineage; however, I have not found any written documentation of this fact. In fact, the 1880 census classified my great-grandparents as Mulatto. Mulattoes were individuals who looked neither Black nor White. In spite of being 'so-called' mulattoes, they understood they were Black and would live as Black individuals. This would often cause division between the lighter-skinned and dark-skinned Negro, which I imagined was the overall intentions of those who thought of this classification.

My grandmother described her mother as having fair skin (meaning light olive skin; today known as copper colored) and she wore her hair in two long, dark braids. Grandmother Florence would share some of those beautiful features. Her wavy, black hair and her olive skin were most complimentary.

The Rainey Sisters

I recall my grandmother Florence talking about her siblings quite a bit. It was oral history that one of her brothers cut hair and had a barber shop on Cedar Street in Pine Bluff, Arkansas. My grandmother Florence also told us of many of the ways of Native American people. She often used many old native herbs to make potions for healing. She knew many of the old prayers and chants. My grandmother was very spiritual and had a peaceful relationship with the Creator. She never talked a lot about her faith but lived it before us.

Aunt Pearlie Rainey Tucker, Grandmother Florence Rainey, Aunt Sally Rainey Knight

Even though I was quite young, I do remember Aunt Emily, Aunt Sally and Aunt Pearlie. My grandmother Florence said the community acknowledged she and her sisters as "The Rainey Sisters" – being born of good looks and raised accordingly. Handsome features were a trait of the Rainey's. They all were of beautiful olive skin and wavy black hair – a Rainey trademark. They were also known in the community for their upbringing and their involvement within their community. My grandmother Florence told us that they formed a church singing group and would sing at different venues. Her brothers had a quartet singing group known as the "Rainey Singers." Grandmother Florence would talk of their singing beautiful quartet harmony. I don't remember having the privilege of hearing their beautiful melodies, since I was so young.

Emily White (Aunt Emily) was the oldest sister. She was taller than Aunt Sallie and my grandmother Florence. She was married and had one daughter, Alonia Douglas, a granddaughter and several great-grandchildren. Her husband passed away before I was born. Aunt Emily was known for her no-nonsense approach about life. One of the stories I heard about Aunt Emily involved a complete stranger who entered Alonia's bedroom through an open window at night in an attempt to assault her. My Aunt Emily entered the room carrying a bat filled with nails. She was quite capable of using her weapon and stopped the attacker in his tracks. Some say he died from the attack. Whatever the case, Aunt Emily protected her daughter. They both would live to discuss it and pass it on.

Pearlie Rainey Tucker (Aunt Pearlie) was much heavier than her three sisters. She may have had a small bone structure at one time but during my childhood I remember her full-size, pleasant figure. Aunt Pearlie married several times but had no natural-born children. She did, however, raise an adopted child. She played the piano. She also owned a grocery store in Gould, Arkansas and was an insurance agent. Aunt Pearlie was known in Gould as a strong community leader, claiming the community in which she lived as the community she would serve. I do remember she went to college in midlife, attending Arkansas Agricultural, Mechanical and Normal College (Arkansas AM&N) which was later incorporated into the University of Arkansas system and renamed the University of Arkansas at Pine Bluff (UAPB). As an adult, she became a college graduate. Even after many years of her passing, she is still remembered and revered in her community. When meeting someone from the area of Gould, Arkansas, I always ask about Miss Pearlie Tucker. "I remember Miss Pearlie Rainey Tucker" is usually the positive response I receive from older individuals who still live in the community.

Aunt Sallie Rainey Knight grew up in the community of Grady but would eventually leave there and make her home in DeWitt, Arkansas. I knew Aunt Sallie as a child. She was very petite like my grandmother Florence. Aunt Sallie must have weighed about 105 pounds. She reminded me of a little doll. She had one daughter and a grandson. They are all gone now.

Even in her eighties, when her hair had turned completely white, Aunt Sallie still had the features of an angel. She wore her wavy hair pulled away from her chiseled face, revealing her beautiful cheekbones. She was known for her beautiful smile and grey eyes.

Aunt Sallie was very much a part of her church and community in DeWitt, Arkansas. The family secret was that during a business meeting at the church, things got out of control. Fingers were pointed, voices were raised and accusations were made. The disagreement ended with my petite, angelic Aunt Sallie assisting the pastor in finding himself on the church floor. This story remains a part of our family. Even today, we are still laughing and smiling about it.

These women, my grandmother and aunts, blazed a trail for me that I am honored to try and follow. These four beautiful Black women, who were classified as Mulattoes, were women of class, strength and solid spirituality. I want to walk out their legacy in my own life. My goal in life has been to not forget them and attempt to embody the same mantle that they possessed, passing their characteristics to my children and grandchildren, praying they will guide them throughout their lives and that they will pass their legacy on to their children and future generations.

ancestry

1900 United States Federal Census

Name:	Cornelias Rainey
Age:	46
Birthplace:	Arkansas
Home in 1900:	Auburn, Lincoln, Arkansas
Race:	Black
Gender:	Male
Relation to Head of House:	Head
Marital Status:	Married
Spouse's Name:	Marthy Rainey
Marriage Year:	1871
Years Married:	29
Father's Birthplace:	Tennessee
Mother's Birthplace:	Tennessee

Household Members:	Name	Age
	Cornelias Rainey	46
	Marthy Rainey	43
	Jim Rainey	20
	Henry Rainey	14
	Lally Rainey	11
	Roger Rainey	8
	Langston Rainey	5
	Pearly Rainey	2

Source Citation: Year: *1900*; Census Place: *Auburn, Lincoln, Arkansas*; Roll: *65*; Page: *5B*; Enumeration District: *0115*; FHL microfilm: *1240065*

Source Information:

THE NATIONAL ARCHIVES ARCHIVES.GOV   Ancestry.com. *1900 United States Federal Census* [database on-line]. Provo, UT, USA: Ancestry.com Operations Inc, 2004. Original Data: United States of America, Bureau of the Census. *Twelfth Census of the United States, 1900.* Washington, D.C.: National Archives and Records Administration, 1900. T623, 1854 rolls.

Description:
This database is an index to individuals enumerated in the 1900 United States Federal Census, the Twelfth Census of the United States. Census takers recorded many details including each person's name, address, relationship to the head of household, color or race, sex, month and year of birth, age at last birthday, marital status, number of years married, the total number of children born of the mother, the number of those children living, birthplace, birthplace of father and mother, if the individual was foreign born, the year of immigration and the number of years in the United States, the citizenship status of foreign-born individuals over age twenty-one, occupation, and more. Additionally, the names of those listed on the population schedule are linked to actual images of the 1900 Federal Census.

1900 Census – Cornelius Rainey

ancestry

1900 United States Federal Census

Name:	Marthy Rainev
Age:	43
Birthplace:	Arkansas
Home in 1900:	Auburn, Lincoln, Arkansas
Race:	Black
Gender:	Female
Relation to Head of House:	Wife
Marital Status:	Married
Spouse's Name:	Cornelias Rainey
Marriage Year:	1871
Years Married:	29
Father's Birthplace:	Virginia
Mother's Birthplace:	Tennessee
Mother: number of living children:	10
Mother: How many children:	15

Household Members:	Name	Age
	Cornelias Rainey	46
	Marthy Rainey	43
	Jim Rainey	20
	Henry Rainey	14
	Lally Rainey	11
	Roger Rainey	8
	Langston Rainey	5
	Pearly Rainey	2

Source Citation: Year: *1900*; Census Place: *Auburn, Lincoln, Arkansas*; Roll: *65*; Page: *5B*; Enumeration District: *0115*; FHL microfilm: *1240065*

Source Information:

Ancestry.com. *1900 United States Federal Census* [database on-line]. Provo, UT, USA: Ancestry.com Operations Inc, 2004.
Original Data: United States of America, Bureau of the Census. *Twelfth Census of the United States, 1900*. Washington, D.C.: National Archives and Records Administration, 1900. T623, 1854 rolls.

Description:
This database is an index to individuals enumerated in the 1900 United States Federal Census, the Twelfth Census of the United States. Census takers recorded many details including each person's name, address, relationship to the head of household, color or race, sex, month and year of birth, age at last birthday, marital status, number of years married, the total number of children born of the mother, the number of those children living, birthplace, birthplace of father and mother, if the individual was foreign born, the year of immigration and the number of years in the United States, the citizenship status of foreign-born individuals over age twenty-one, occupation, and more. Additionally, the names of those listed on the population schedule are linked to actual images of the 1900 Federal Census.

1880 Census – Martha Rainey

ancestry

1880 United States Federal Census

Name:	Florence Rainey
Age:	5
Birth Year:	abt 1875
Birthplace:	Arkansas
Home in 1880:	Auburn, Lincoln, Arkansas
Race:	Mulatto
Gender:	Female
Relation to Head of House:	Daughter
Marital Status:	Single
Father's Name:	Cornelius Rainey
Father's Birthplace:	Arkansas
Mother's Name:	Martha Rainey
Mother's Birthplace:	Arkansas
Occupation:	Laborer

Household Members:	Name	Age
	Cornelius Rainey	35
	Martha Rainey	26
	Emma Rainey	9
	Sampson Rainey	7
	Florence Rainey	5

Source Citation: Year: *1880*; Census Place: *Auburn, Lincoln, Arkansas*; Roll: *49*; Family History Film: *1254049*; Page: *16A*; Enumeration District: *174*; Image: *0579*

Source Information:

Ancestry.com and The Church of Jesus Christ of Latter-day Saints. *1880 United States Federal Census* [database on-line]. Provo, UT, USA: Ancestry.com Operations Inc, 2010. 1880 U.S. Census Index provided by The Church of Jesus Christ of Latter-day Saints © Copyright 1999 Intellectual Reserve, Inc. All rights reserved. All use is subject to the limited use license and other terms and conditions applicable to this site.

Original Data: Tenth Census of the United States, 1880. (NARA microfilm publication T9, 1,454 rolls). Records of the Bureau of the Census, Record Group 29. National Archives, Washington, D.C.

Description:
This database is an index to 50 million individuals enumerated in the 1880 United States Federal Census. Census takers recorded many details including each person's name, address, occupation, relationship to the head of household, race, sex, age at last birthday, marital status, place of birth, parents' place of birth. Additionally, the names of those listed on the population schedule are linked to actual images of the 1880 Federal Census.

1880 Census – Florence Rainey

Chapter 2

Our Grandmother – Florence Rainey Liggions Lamb

"And now, Israel, what doth the Lord require of thee,
but to fear the Lord our God, to walk in all His ways,
and to love Him, and to serve the Lord thy God with all
thy heart and with all thy soul."

Deuteronomy 10:12

Grandmother Florence and Mr. Liggions

Grandmother Florence was born in 1906 in Vaugine, Jefferson County, Arkansas. She was one of the most saintly, peaceful, and loving woman I have ever known. She was a petite, very soft spoken lady with a beautiful olive complexion, coupled with a serene smile. Behind that smile, observing you closely, were the kindest soft grey eyes. Most of us called her Grandma. To many others who revered her, she was called "Mother Lamb." Her beautiful smile always put you at ease; never judging you or condemning you. Her words were always healing and few.

For a short period of time, Grandmother Florence had been married to a Mr. Liggions and one son, Wallace Liggions, was born to that union. After Mr. Liggions passed away, Grandmother Florence married John Lamb in 1892. Bible records verify this. Grandfather Lamb would raise Wallace Liggions as his own son.

At a very young age, Wallace would join the military. I recall Grandmother Florence telling us, as children, that Uncle Wallace was living in Wilberforce, Ohio. I do recall her saying that she once went to Wilberforce, Ohio to visit him. He was probably stationed there at the time.

Uncle Wallace would eventually marry and to that union a daughter named Lorraine Liggions, was born. Many years later, Uncle Wallace would die in a car accident. I believe it was in Wilberforce, Ohio. According to oral family history, years later, his wife, Elizabeth, was also killed in a car accident.

Uncle Wallace's daughter, Lorraine Liggions, was a professional woman. She married a white gentleman, Mr. Peter Bolander. They had a daughter. Tragically, Lorraine and her daughter would also die in a car accident in Chicago in 1969. She was only 26 years old. Her husband was not in the car at the time of the accident.

Lorraine Liggions Bolander

Lorraine received a Bachelor of Science Degree in Mathematics from the Illinois Institute of Technology (ITT) in 1953 and a Masters Degree in Applied Mathematics from DePaul University in 1954.

At the time of her death she was employed at the Arthur D. Little, Inc. prior to that, she worked as a mathematician for IBM and at Massachusetts General Hospital where she taught computer and introduced mathematical and computer techniques as research to doctors.

Lorraine Liggions Bolander

As of this writing, Lorraine's husband, Mr. Bolander, is living on the east coast. He and my oldest brother, Wallace Johnson, would meet for the first time in 2016. Both men are now in their mid-eighties.

Grandmother Florence & John Lamb

According to the United States Census, Grandmother Florence would marry John Lamb in 1892. Bible records also verify this date. She married at 17 years of age. My grandfather John was 18 to 20 years older. Oral history in our family called her a child bride because of her youth.

Grandfather John Lamb was born in South Carolina. He was of a small frame, chestnut skin tone, handsome, with a gentle demeanor. He was known as a gentleman who commanded respect.

After his first wife died in South Carolina, he traveled to Arkansas with several children. Oral history states that some of the children he brought to Arkansas were older, and/or the same age as my grandmother Florence. After moving to Arkansas, several of them continued to live with their father and were raised by he and grandmother Florence. Several of the children would pass away shortly after coming to Arkansas. One daughter named Hattie was often mentioned by my mother as one of the children that lived to elderly years.

I'm sure there must have been challenges, raising young adults. However, due to the times in which they lived, different value systems, and family connections, they were able to overcome those hurdles. Grandfather John and grandmother Florence would have seven children together.

My mother always told us that grandfather Lamb treated grandmother Florence with much love and respect requiring others to respect her as well. My mother and grandmother often stated that he demanded respect from Whites as well as Blacks. "His word was his bond" has been repeated throughout my family, as often as I can remember.

He was known to respect all and expected the same respect from others.

Grandmother Florence

It is said that when my grandfather married my grandmother, he carried her to the local mercantile store and introduced her as his wife and said "This is my wife, Mrs. Lamb" because of her young, innocent looks. He required respect for her from the owner of the Mercantile store, who was white, where he gave authorization to my grandmother to sign grandfather Lamb's name, for credit, as Mrs. Lamb. This level of respect for my grandparents would remain throughout their lives within their community.

Eight years later, the following children were listed in the 1900 census as living with John and Florence Lamb:

Hattie Lamb (14 years)
Wallace Lamb (9 years)
McKinley Lamb (4 years)
Luther Lamb (3 years)

Oral history within the family says that our grandfather, John Lamb, was a brick mason in Pine Bluff, Arkansas. Although I have not been able to find any records that support this, my mother, Victoria Lamb Carroll verified his trade as a brick mason.

Grandfather John worked and laid many of the bricks on buildings in Pine Bluff, Arkansas. Many of them are still standing today in downtown Pine Bluff. I believe that my grandfather John Lamb helped in erecting many of those building from the early 1800's. So much of the history of Pine Bluff has been lost; however, a great deal of our history is being discovered.

Grandfather Lamb would pass own before I was born; however, how he lived his life is still quite alive within our family. I grew up hearing about the giant of a man that grandfather was. He lived a very principled life. We were told that he lived by giving and receiving respect from the community.

My four older siblings; Wallace, Darlean, Doris, and Myrtle have memories of our grandfather. When they were born, he was already up in age. I wish I could have known him. The way he took care of my grandmother, and the love he demonstrated to she and the family. He was truly a family man, a man of character, an astute gentleman, one who stood out in his community. He would leave a beautiful legacy to the men in our family.

My grandparents and great grandparents were of the Christian faith. They would practice the teachings of Jesus Christ, within the Baptist Church, and throughout their community. The little church my parents and grandparents attended while living in Grady, Arkansas, Pleasant Grove Baptist Church, is still standing today. It is located on 1520 Dakota Road in Grady, Arkansas, about ten to fifteen minutes outside of Pine Bluff, headed east. A mile down Dakota Road, you will arrive at this little white brick church which is surrounded by cotton and rice fields. Although the church has been remodeled, it still has the old historical marker, a large old bell that rests on the grounds of this small community church. A warm, serene feeling engulfs you as soon as you step onto the soil. You feel so far away from the noise and the hustle and bustle from the city - you are transported back in time. You feel a sense of peace and serenity. A sense that after all your travel you are finally returning home to a place, that is quiet, embracing, and reminder of the past. My grandmother often talked of Grady, Arkansas.

I can only imagine the wonderful fellowship they must have had while experiencing the mighty move of their God. The God that would give them the peace, comfort and strength they would need, through the many challenges they must have faced. That spirit of love and fellowship and belonging still thrives in that community. Even today, this small rural church is still attended by some of the children of the older generations.

I recall the strong spiritual connection they would pass on to the family. Watching their lives, how they lived, how they honored and served a Living God. Growing up under their watchful eyes would lay a foundation that would be a strong legacy to the family. Our God would become so real to us because of the lives our grand-parents and loved ones lived before us. Our roots were definitely rooted in the knowledge of God, the Creator of heaven and earth. Worship was a part of our rearing, and has remained with the family. The legacy of John Lamb and Cornelius Rainey have been woven throughout our family. *All praise to the Most High!*

Most of the family is buried in Pleasant Grove Cemetery which is located in plain view behind the church. The grounds are cov-ered with beautiful head stones and monuments. Nestled among the trees and the open fields rest my mother, Victoria, Grandma Florence, Grandpa John Lamb, my Uncle Wallace Liggions, my Aunt Gertie Lamb Wynne, and her daughter, Geraldine Wynne

Connors. Their wishes were to return to their place of birth, and their requests were honored. Other families that are resting there are the Holmes, and the Wynnes to whom we are related, and other families that I have only heard of. The small community of Grady, Arkansas, holds the remains and spirits of many African Americans and their loved ones of that era. My Uncle Luther Lamb and Uncle Johnnie Lamb, being veterans, are buried in the Veterans Cemetery in Little Rock, Arkansas.

The grounds are very well maintained by the church. Donations from family members who have love ones there are accepted. I try to visit as often as I can. My roots are tied to Pine Bluff and Grady, Arkansas, though I currently live at neither.

Oral history has given us such a clear and abiding history of this little community. Their roots are deeply woven in Christian values. The oral history and fellowship has been kept alive. The history passed on to many of us, depict people, many of whom were poor sharecroppers. Many of them worked their own land. Others struggled to exist. However, their faith in a living God and their hope in the future kept families in tack and pushed them forward.

My ancestors were able to forge out a meager living, farming, sharecropping, chopping cotton and soybeans. I applaud their survival and their living faith, a faith that has brought me through many dangerous toils and shares, a faith that demonstrated to me how to keep going in the midst of hard ships and injustices. Working the land but never owning it. Many remained in debt to the owners of the land. Few were ever able to save and purchase their own land.

Oral history says that Grandmother Florence and Grandfather John at some point did own property on old Princeton Pike, in Pine Bluff, Arkansas. However, some misfortune caused a loss of that property.

My mother, Victoria, was in her sixties before she was able to purchase a home for the family. By this time, my father was not in the home, however he did contribute to the purchasing of our first home in Pine Bluff, Arkansas at 703 Missouri Street.

ancestry

1900 United States Federal Census

Name:	John Lamb
Age:	43
Birthplace:	South Carolina
Home in 1900:	Vaugine, Jefferson, Arkansas
Race:	Black
Gender:	Male
Relation to Head of House:	Head
Marital Status:	Married
Spouse's Name:	Florence Lamb
Marriage Year:	1892
Years Married:	8
Father's Birthplace:	South Carolina
Mother's Birthplace:	South Carolina

Household Members:	Name	Age
	John Lamb	43
	Florence Lamb	25
	Wallace Lamb	9
	Mckiney Lamb	4
	Luther Lamb	3
	Hattie Lamb	14

Source Citation: Year: *1900*; Census Place: *Vaugine, Jefferson, Arkansas*; Roll: *63*; Page: *25B*; Enumeration District: *0098*; FHL microfilm: *1240063*

Source Information:

Ancestry.com. *1900 United States Federal Census* [database on-line]. Provo, UT, USA: Ancestry.com Operations Inc, 2004.
Original Data: United States of America, Bureau of the Census. *Twelfth Census of the United States,* *1900.* Washington, D.C.: National Archives and Records Administration, 1900. T623, 1854 rolls.

Description:
This database is an index to individuals enumerated in the 1900 United States Federal Census, the Twelfth Census of the United States. Census takers recorded many details including each person's name, address, relationship to the head of household, color or race, sex, month and year of birth, age at last birthday, marital status, number of years married, the total number of children born of the mother, the number of those children living, birthplace, birthplace of father and mother, if the individual was foreign born, the year of immigration and the number of years in the United States, the citizenship status of foreign-born individuals over age twenty-one, occupation, and more. Additionally, the names of those listed on the population schedule are linked to actual images of the 1900 Federal Census.

Chapter 3

The Children of John and Florence Lamb

"And I will betroth thee onto me forever, yea, I will betroth thee unto me in righteousness, and in judgement, and in loving kindness, and in mercies. I will even betroth thee unto me in faithfulness; and thou shall know the Lord."

Hosea 2:19-20

According to the 1910 United States Federal Census, John Lamb was 50 years old and Florence was 34 years of age. Children in the home were: McKinley Lamb (13 years), Luther Lamb (11 years), Beatrice Lamb (8 years), Johnie Lamb (5 years), Florence Lamb [Aunt Tonsy] (4 years), and Gertie Lamb (1 year).

McKinley

McKinley was the first child born to this union. I recall his name being mentioned while growing up. I loved the sound of the name McKinley. The sound of his name was spellbinding to my young ears. I could imagine he was very handsome and astute since my grandmother was so angelic in appearance and in character and my grandfather, a gentle and strong man.

When McKinley reached adulthood he left the clan in Grady, Arkansas. He traveled to another state. We were told that McKinley had met with some success and that he had a shoe shop in Kansas. I don't know if McKinley was married, or had children. He invited our grandmother to come and live with him. At this time, she and my grandfather Lamb had purchased a home located outside of the city of Pine Bluff, Arkansas in an area called Princeton Pike. My grandmother would sell her home. We were told a local white doctor purchased the home. I don't know all the details surrounding my grandmother losing her home following the passing of Grandfather Lamb.

Upon arrival, however, she discovered that McKinley's story did not match up to what he had told her. She would eventually return to Pine Bluff, Arkansas, but she no longer owned the home out in the Princeton Pike area.

Luther

I met Uncle Luther on many occasions. He had a very strong presence. His skin was a beautiful copper color, with piercing eyes and a stare that indicated at all times that he was a man on the move and was not about laughter and small talk. He was connected with law enforcement in Little Rock, Arkansas.

I recall he often came to Pine Bluff to visit Grandmother Florence. It was always on Sunday after church. At this time grandmother was living in our home. She was now in her 70's and my mother did not want her to live alone, after Grandpa Lamb had passed on. When Uncle Luther would visit, we were always in awe of him. We did not want to be in his view. His looks were piercing and would make you feel quite uneasy. I can see Uncle Luther walking through the door in his black felt hat and his long black wool overcoat. We would clear the room. He never brought my grandmother anything as I recall. It was rumored that he carried his weapon at all times.

It was also known that he never forgave my grandmother for putting him out of the home as a young man. We were told that he did not want to adhere to their rules.It is said that grandma packed his suitcase and set it out on the curve. The instructions were *"Take either end of the road you desire."* Uncle Luther would leave the home and chart his own path in life. I understand that he would carry this anger for the remaining of his life.

It is also rumored that he threatened to kill one of my older sisters who spoke to him in a playful manner. After his threat, she cried and forever stayed out of his sight. Therefore we, as young children and young adults, knew to stay clear of him. We had great respect for him, to no surprise. We really feared him.

Uncle Luther never had children. However, he did marry a very nice lady, who was very tall in stature, named Aunt Lou. She was always very cordial toward us and we always enjoyed her presence. I do recall Uncle Luther's passing on. I believe he would pass before our grandmother in Little Rock, Arkansas. Grandpa had passed on many years prior.

Beatrice

Beatrice Lamb Willis was the oldest daughter of John and Florence's eight children. We were told she looked like Grandpa Lamb, a beautiful woman, petite in size and chestnut in complexion. She was full of charisma and energy

Aunt Bee, as we called her, married at a very early age. She would marry Mr. Willis, whom she called "Babe," and became the mother of 12 children. She was a stay at home mother and truly a very strong Christian woman. She was known for her strong hand and belief in not sparing the rod.

Aunt Beatrice, being the oldest girl and my mother Victoria, who was the youngest, were very close. Although Aunt Bee lived in Little

Rock she would visit grandmother as often as she could which I recall being very frequently. A family member would always bring her down to Pine Bluff. They also visited on the telephone often. I do not recall them being estranged from each other. They maintained their bond all of their lives.

Aunt Beatrice would live to be in her eighties. As she got older and could not live alone, she would move to Los Angeles, California with one of her children. She would pass away in California. Aunt Bee would be returned to Little Rock, Arkansas for her final resting place. Aunt Beatrice was buried in the Veteran's Cemetery next to her husband and other family members.

As of 2016, Aunt Beatrice has one daughter living in Los Angeles, California, and several grandchildren and great grandchildren. She leaves a legacy of fond memories and life lessons. I currently remain in close contact with many of her grandchildren and great grandchild.

Aunt Florence ("Tonsey")

Aunt Florence Lamb Young, who we called Aunt Tonsey lived in Kansas City, Missouri. According to census records of 1910, Aunt Florence was named after her mother, Florence Lamb. She was a beautiful woman. Aunt Tonsey gave birth to one child, name Marie. Marie and H. L. McKenley, had two children, Pat and Lawrence. I believe they are living in Kansas City, Kansas today.

Aunt Florence looked more like her mother Florence. She was olive in complexion. I recall Aunt Tonsey had silver, curly hair. I always enjoyed her coming to our home to visit Grandma. She would always come by train, and would stay for one or two weeks. She and my mother shared a very close relationship throughout their lives. Aunt Tonsey had these beautiful grey eyes, with a very warm smile. When her visit was over, I would hate to see her go home to Kansas.

Aunt Tonsey would live out her life in Kansas and would be buried in Kansas. Her grandchildren, Pat and Lawrence, would often travel with her. After her death, they never returned to Pine Bluff, nor have I seen either of them since Aunt Tonsey's passing.

Johnnie Lamb

In 1910 Uncle Johnnie Lamb was five years old. Uncle Johnnie, as we called him, was my mother's youngest brother. His name was John Lamb, after his father. Uncle Johnnie was an astute gentle man, like his dad. He was very handsome with straight silver hair. Uncle Johnnie, had light colored eyes like his mother, and an olive complexion.

My mother, Victoria and her brother Johnnie, always had a warm relationship. My mother always made them welcome, to her home. Uncle Johnnie and Aunt Lou, never had children. They seem to be a very happy couple.

Aunt Gertrude ("Aunt Gurtie")

My Aunt Gertude Lamb Wynne; whom we called Aunt Gertie married Rev. Kerry Wynne, a preacher. She was a beautiful woman, like her mother. She owned and operated a community store in her neighborhood of Pine Bluff, Arkansas. She was a Christian woman and a leader in her community. Her husband, who we called Uncle Kerry, spent many years preaching the gospel. Aunt Gertie, as well as her other siblings, would make numerous trips to our home to visit her mother, Florence.

Aunt Gertie and Uncle Kerry had two children: Gerldine and Kerry. Their daughter, Gerldine Wynne Connor, would teach for many years at Dollarway High School in Pine Bluff, Arkansas, later teaching out-of-state before her retirement. Aunt Gertie's second child, Rev. Dr Kerry Wynne, Jr., a well-known minister of the Gospel, and former professor of Morehead College. Aunt Gertie had no grandchildren.

As children, we loved visiting our Aunt Gertie Wynne and spending many weeks at their home. We enjoyed being in her home. She was kind and was always happy to have us spend the night. Her home was the first home, that I recall, being able to sit and watch television. We did not own a television and would enjoy the visits. I recall playing in her son Kerry's sandbox and riding his bicycle. Her home was always warm and pleasant.

Aunt Gertie would live well into her eighties in the care of her two children. Upon her death in 2000, she would also be buried in Grady, Arkansas alongside other family members. Upon his death, I believe Uncle Kerry was also buried in Grady, Arkansas, along with their daughter, Ms. Gerldine Wynne.

My mother, Victoria, and her sister Gertie differed in the care of my grandmother. I never understood their differences. My mother loved her sister, and often told us as children she would cry to go to her big sister's home and be with her. She missed her so desperately, following her marriage and leaving the home. My mother, being the baby, would be the last one to leave the Lamb home.

Chapter 4

⋯⊰❖⊱⋯

Grandmother's Last Years

"When thou passed through the waters, I will be with thee, and through the rivers, they shall not over-flow thee; when thou walkest through the fire, thou shall not be burned; neither shall the flame kindle upon thee."

Isaiah 43:2

Grandmother Florence always lived in close proximity to our family. However, after she began to get older and in failing health, my mother, being the youngest of her siblings, brought her to live in our home. We loved being close to our grandmother. She was a beautiful, gentle woman. We loved her dearly. We loved having our grandmother near us. We spent as much time with her as we could. At some point, all of my siblings lived with my grandmother. We would squabble as to who would spend the night with Grandma Florence.

Her home was always quiet and peaceful. Grandma had an extra room, with a little iron cot. I remember the little metal frame cot. The quietness of the little shotgun house, was like being in heaven. It was always joyful to get away from the hustle and bustle of being home with my siblings. We children had the same idea. We wanted to stay with grandma as often as we could. She never scolded us.

She spoke very infrequently to us. Quietness was the norm for us children whenever we were around our grandmother. We willingly followed the rules, just to be in her presence was a delight. As children, we just loved to be in her presence. We loved her dearly, and wanted to be there for her.

All of my grandmother's children would usually visit her on Sundays. Most of Uncle Johnnie's visits would be on Sunday after church. He, too, would dress in his long black overcoat, with a black felt hat. He was kind, and his wife, Aunt Lou, would always accompany him to our home. Both of our uncles' wives were named Lou!

During this time, my grandmother had gotten up in age. They would come and go to her bedroom. She would sit in her black rocking chair or recline in her bed. They would talk with her for a short while and then leave. They would never stay long enough to tire her out, nor would they take her from the house. I don't recall them bringing gifts to her, or feeling too comfortable. I'm sure those visits meant a lot to her. As a child, I respected them, and we stayed quiet and out of the way while my mother's siblings visited their mother.

When grandma moved into our home, my mother brought her own furniture to our home. Her room was at the rear of our home, near the bathroom. Her room was comfortable with beautiful curtains, rugs and pictures on the walls. My mother made it very comfortable for her.

Grandma had this old black Singer Sewing Machine with a floor peddle. I loved going through the drawers of the old Singer machine. Those drawers contained wonderful little trinkets. When peeping in the drawers or looking for something for grandma, my eyes would behold bobbins, spools of thread, needles, coins, thimbles, scissors, all types of little items pertaining to sewing. I recall a little bottle of Carter's Little liver pills. Everything was a little treasure.

Grandma also had this beautiful brown mahogany bedroom set. It was accompanied with a large dresser with a large mirror. Across the room was her large black trunk which contained the beautiful quilts she and her sister Emily had made - quilts that they had spent many hours, weeks, months and years quilting.

Quilting frames, or quilting horses as they were commonly called, were used to make the quilts. Two - six to eight feet poles were placed adjacent to each other. These two poles were placed atop, what was called horses. The frames were made in the shape of a horse, with legs, which would support the poles on top.

The poles were positioned about arm's length, from the person sitting on either side of the frame. The objective was each individual could work on one side, about-facing the other individual. Working arm's length from the other. As a section was completed, the poles were moved, revealing sections of the quilts that had not been stitched to the matting. The quilting horses were made of wood and were put away at the end of quilting season.

Grandma and Aunt Emily used very colorful soft cotton scrapes of fabrics. Some fabrics were old clothing that was worn out, from years of wear. The heavier comforters were made from old scraps of wools that were no longer in use. Their quilts were quilted by hand. The small stitches were sewn with strong white thread. I marveled at the small stiches, the straight lines, in which the stiches were kept, sometime curving them and creating a pattern of stiches. These patterns were sewn together by hand, demonstrating unique skill and were called the quilt tops. After completion of all the designs together, they were sewn to an all cream or white fabric call muslin material which was soft and added the finishing touches to the quilt tops. Between the matting or backing, soft cotton was placed between top and bottom. This process would go on for hours, days and weeks, before a finished piece of artwork was revealed.

Many, many hours, my sister Vernett and I sat under those quilting horses, quiet as a mouse, as grandmother and her sister Emily quilted on, late iinto the evening. When my grandmother and her sister spoke, they would speak very softly. We knew not to disturb them in any way. They never raised their voices. An entire day of quilting would end. We would walk home at the end of the quilting day, elated from having been in the presence of such quiet, beautiful women. Grandmother Florence always wore a hat, accompanied by an apron and a tiny white lace handkerchief in her apron pocket. Quilting would begin the next day, like clockwork.

Vernett and Vivian

As a child, I never recalled these sisters dishonoring a friend or neighbor, or gossiping concerning someone else. They definitely minded their own business. We never heard the use of profanity or any other idle communication. They were beautiful gentile women of that era. Occasionally, they would mention the church or the blessings of God. They were very much women of God and practiced their faith.

Grandmother and her sister would make the most beautiful quilts. Each quilt would have a name; such as "Ring Around the Roses," and "Jacob's ladder." "The Star of David" was my favorite of all of their quilts. They created a beautiful quilt called "Orion The Hunter."

Most of these quilts were made for a full-size bed. Many were large enough that they could drape over the side of the bed. To my knowledge, they did not quilt twin size quilts. Whatever size they created, they were most beautiful, done with love, and were beautiful pieces of art.

As a child, I did not realize the beauty and charm of those quilts. Several of these quilts would remain in our home long after my grandmother had passed away. Unfortunately, I did not inherit one of those priceless treasures. They seem to have disappeared through the years. I regret that I never owned one of these treasures from the past. Somewhere they are being used to warm and to comfort a family member. Many blessings to whoever owns them today.

Using grandma's techniques and patience, I, too, have made small quilts for my children and grandchildren. They do not compare to my grandma's and her sister's quilts. I could not duplicate their talent and patience.

According to Proverbs 31;1, these were truly women of grace, creativity, peace, and charm. During hours of quilting, grandma and her sister, never indulged in small talk or gossip. These women had beauty, charm, faith, and deep abiding spirituality and maintained an atmosphere of peace and tranquility. They cheerfully allowed the Creator, to Bless the works of their hands, as He had promised. They were definitely the Proverb 31 Women!

> *Who can find a virtuous woman? for her price is far above rubies. The heart of her husband doth safely trust in her, so that he shall have no need of spoil. She will do him good and not evil all the days of her life.*
>
> *She seeketh wool, and flax, and worketh willingly with her hands. She is like the merchants' ships; she bringeth her food from afar. She riseth also while it is yet night, and giveth meat to her household, and a portion to her maidens.*
>
> *She considereth a field, and buyeth it: with the fruit of her hands she planteth a vineyard. She girdeth her loins with strength, and strengtheneth her arms. She perceiveth that her merchandise is good: her candle goeth not out by night. She layeth her hands to the spindle, and her hands hold the distaff. She stretcheth out her hand to the poor; yea, she reacheth forth her hands to the needy.*
>
> *She is not afraid of the snow for her household: for all her household are clothed with scarlet. She maketh herself coverings of tapestry; her clothing is silk and purple. Her husband is known in the gates, when he sitteth among the elders of the land. She maketh fine linen, and selleth it; and delivereth girdles unto the merchant.*

Strength and honour are her clothing; and she shall rejoice in time to come. She openeth her mouth with wisdom; and in her tongue is the law of kindness. She looketh well to the ways of her household, and eateth not the bread of idleness. Her children arise up, and call her blessed; her husband also, and he praiseth her.

Many daughters have done virtuously, but thou excellest them all. Favour is deceitful, and beauty is vain: but a woman that feareth the LORD, she shall be praised.Give her of the fruit of her hands; and let her own works praise her in the gates. [Proverbs 31:10-31 KJV]

Grandmother Lamb would live to 101 years and would pass from a brief illness which the doctor diagnosed as old age. She would leave this earth very peacefully and full of conviction that she would meet her Maker, face-to-face.

I cannot express the love, honor, reverence, and respect I held for my grandmother. We loved her presence. I never tired of or regretted being asked to look in on her, or to prepare her food, whatever I could do for her. I felt only love, wanting to be around her.

To my siblings and me, our grandmother Florence, shaped our lives in many ways. I thank God for her time on this earth, and in our lives. We children shared in her daily care when she had gotten up in age. We made her bed, combed her hair, brought her food, cleaned her small room, helped with her every need. We demonstrated our love, whenever we had the opportunity.

Chapter 5

Our Mother: Victoria Lamb

"For the eyes of the Lord run to and fro throughout the whole earth, to shew himself strong in the behalf of them whose heart is perfect toward Him.

II Chronicles 16:9

John and Florence would have one more child, my mother, Victoria Lamb. She is listed in the 1920's United States Census Records as being four years of age which means she would have been born in 1916. When she was born, Grandpa John Lamb was 60, and Grandma Florence was 35 years old.

My mother, Victoria Lamb Carroll

My mother, Victoria was a beautiful, petite woman of soft chestnut complexion. She was vivacious, smart with a strong willingness to get things done that needed to be done for her family. Growing up in such a large family and being the youngest of eight children, with three older brothers, (my Uncles Wallace, Luther and Johnnie) must have been quite rewarding, with many experiences, and attention. She would know courage, wit, fortitude and very strong faith.

My mother never talked a lot about her childhood. I do recall her being educated to the eighth grade. During those early years, many young people were only educated to eighth grade. Many poor families kept their children home to work the crops and the fields. Education was truly a luxury for most Black families.

My mother, Victoria Lamb Carroll, was known for her academic abilities, and became a teacher very early. She would teach the other young children in the community. According to oral history, she was the community teacher in Grady, Arkansas and was known to be smart, capable, and a self-starter. Although she had been prepared to raise ten children and the wife of three husbands, she did not realize how difficult and challenging her life would be.

Our mother was a strong disciplinarian. I recall anger and many harsh whippings. Now that I am 70, I can understand why. I understand her pain, her disappointments in life, the many hardships and challenges she would experience in life - raising 10 children without a constant father in the home; marrying three men, hoping life would improve only to experience increased challenges and stress. I watched her struggle, working two jobs. I recall her working one job before going to the next job, trying to provide for her family.

I don't recall my mother complaining as to her lot in life. She was angry, tired, and had to take so much abuse in her own life. This, I imagine, would create such feelings of hurt, because of her unfulfilled dreams and expectations. In spite of the number of children and hopeful mates, she would press on and accept the conditions she found herself in. There would be no one to rescue her from her lot in life. Her only rescue would be her faith in her God, and the coming together in her church. There she would be able to vent her soul, and let her burdens go. Mother's favorite verse was in Psalms 71:

> "In thee, O Lord, do I put my trust; let me never be put to shame. Be thou my strong habitation, which unto I may continually rest; Thou has given commandments to save me, for Thou art my rock and my fortune. Cast me not off in the time of old age; forsake me not when my strength fail me. Now also when I am old and grey headed. God forsake me not, until I have showed thy strength unto this generation and thy power to everyone who is to come."

I recall on Sunday mornings, while she prepared breakfast for us, she would manage to get a good cry in. She often cried as she would listen to Mahalia Jackson, the African-American gospel singer. I could imagine, hearing those old spirituals, would lift her spirits, and she would feel that tomorrow would be better. I would watch this ritual every Sunday morning. My mother had so much faith in her God that she just kept on going. At 73 years of age her faith in her God never waivered nor was she ever without hope.

Even though she was the youngest of Grandma Florence's children, my mother, Victoria, would not see longevity of years. Grandma Florence would live to 101 years. Our mother would only live to be 73 years of age. Her life was short compared to her mother Florence, her aunts, sisters and her four older children who are now in their

80's. My mother would suffer from high blood pressure, stress and renal failure. She would never realize the lifestyle, or the wishes, she so desired. She wanted a mate and a provider. Her Church, her God, and her ten children that she worked so hard to raise, would be her treasures in life. I truly hope they were enough for her.

Chapter 6

Victoria and Levi Johnson

For the LORD WILL NOT FORSAKE HIS PEOPLE
FOR HIS GREAT NAME'S SAKE:
BECAUSE IT HATH PLEASED THE LORD TO MAKE YOU
HIS PEOPLE.

I Samuel 12:22

My mother's first marriage was to a Mr. Auther. According to oral history, the marriage was short lived. Mother would later marry Levi Johnson. This marriage would produce four children: Wallace Johnson, the oldest, Darlean, Doris, and Myrtle Johnson. However, their marriage ended in divorce. As of this writing, my four older siblings are in their eighties, and are in good health.

Mr. Johnson would move to Fort Wayne, Indiana. He would leave the marriage and three children behind. At the time our mother, Victoria, would be pregnant with her fourth child. Oral history said that mother did not know her husband was planning on leaving the family - not while she was carrying their fourth child.

I recall our mother telling us that on the morning of his departure she observed him dressing in several layers of clothes. She watched as he dressed and left the home. She did not question him as to his intention. He was gone from her life, and the lives of their children. Several days later, he would return to the home with the authorities and retrieve the mattress, pillows, and bed that her mother Florence had given them as a wedding gift.

The Children of Victoria and Levi Johnson
Wallace Johnson

After Wallace was born, my mother secured a job in Pine Bluff which was about 20 miles away from home. She would return home to Grady, Arkansas often. However, her oldest son, Wallace, would be left in the care of my Grandma Florence and Grandpa John Lamb. During that time, tradition was if a child was born in the grandparents' home, and the mother left the home, for whatever reason, the mother would leave the child behind in the grandparents care, the home in which they were born.

Wallace, her first born, would learn to call our mother 'Sister' instead of Mother. He was mostly raised by our grandmother and this would shape his life very early. His young ears heard his mother being called Sister therefore he, too, would call her 'Sister' all of her life. Mama never expressed her feelings about this. I imagined she wanted to be called mother or mama. While I was growing up, I would hear him call her Sister when he would come home to visit. It would sound so foreign to my ears. All of his siblings called her mom, or mama, or Ma'dear.

Wallace, being the older brother, always stood head and shoulders above the rest of his siblings. He was very astute and focused. We looked up to him as an older brother. He was never unkind to us. We would remain in awe of him, and even today, at 87 years of age.

While in college, Wallace worked at W. D. Wells Typewriter Company. I never knew what he did. I do recall he had a Royal typewriter in his room. Wallace had his own room. He would remind us as his young siblings not to go in his room. Of course we would find a way into his room, even with the inside door being locked.

We would enter through the rear door that led to the outside. We loved to peck on the typewriter, and browse through his belongings. We would make sure we did not leave any clues that we had been in his room, snooping around.

Wallace would enter the United States Air Force and travel to Japan, where he would remain for at least two years. We missed him deeply, as our older brother. Upon his return, Wallace would get back to his post of being the older brother. Our mother Victoria, often told us that our brother Wallace bought the first bed that we younger children slept on. I understand that Wallace sent his military check home to our mother each month. Wallace was known for saving his money while in the Air Force. Wallace's allotment each month would purchase our first television set. Wallace never spoke of these things to his siblings. This would be told to us by our mother. This made us very proud of our brother.

After military life, Wallace would return to Arkansas and complete his college education at Arkansas Agricultural, Mechanical and Normal College (Arkansas AM&N) in Pine Bluff earning a degree in Business Administration. There Wallace would meet and marry Anne Calloway, who was also a student there.

Wallace and Anne have been married for over 50 years. They reside in Seattle, Washington and have three children: Stephen, Regenia and Cecilia, and six grandchildren.

As of this writing in 2018, Wallace is 87 years of age. He is still very active, and very engaged in his community and church life. According to Anne, his wife, he is in much demand at his age, being a man of God, with very high principles and a real gentleman.

Wallace was the backbone of our family. He made our lives better by sending home his allotment from the military. He is still caring for his siblings even now. He still calls all of his siblings on special days and holidays with words of encouragement. I recall he recently came to visit all of his siblings and spent three days with me in my home.

Darlean, Doris, and Myrtle would be the next in line to leave home. They, too, would make their marks in life. They would marry and have children, grandchildren and great grandchildren. They are in their eighties, and in good health. Some have lost children through death, and have faced and overcome many challenges throughout their lives. We have all added more to the Rainey, Lamb, Johnson, and Carroll clans.

Darlean Johnson Curry

Darlean Johnson Curry, the second oldest sibling of the family is 85 years of age at this writing. Darlean would be the second sibling to leave the home. Upon graduating from Merrill High School in Pine Bluff, Arkansas she moved to Fort Wayne, Indiana where her father, Levi Johnson, lived. This is where she would make her home for over sixty-five years.

Darlean, a beautiful young woman with chestnut skin and beautiful shoulder length black hair, would marry Josephe Curry of Fort Wayne, Indiana. to that union were born six children; Josephe Curry Jr., James Curry, Debra Kaye Curry, Tommy and Shelia Curry. Five of Darlean's children would leave this earth's realm before their mother. As of this writing, one child, Sheila Curry, is still living.

My sister has had great sorrow in her life. However her faith in God has kept her strong. She has never questioned God, as to why her husband and her children would precede her in this life. Jesus reminds us that he won't leave us, nor will He forsake us. He will go with us, all the days of our lives. His word is true. I have such admiration for Darlean's faith and her ability to keep on going. I often tell her she is a light, a wonderful mother, grandmother and woman of God. Darlean is still a beautiful woman, and very active in her church. She still travels and drives her own car.

She has many grandchildren and great-grandchildren. They love her dearly. We attempted to tabulate over the telephone the number of her offspring. We concluded with much to little success, five generations. Darlene has 24 grandchildren, 22 great-grandchildren, and three great-great-grandchildren.

Doris Johnson, K'nuckles, Duncans

Doris would leave home following high school graduation, also. She would marry Louis K'Nuckles. To their union was born Louis K'Nuckles, Jr., Timothy K'Nuckles, Shirley and Joe K'Nuckles. Joe Daryl, as we called him, passed several years ago.

As of this writing, Doris is in good health at 83 years of age. She is a lovely woman with an olive-brown complexion and shoulder length, beautiful black hair. Doris, recently retired after working 50 years in the Pine Bluff School District. She was secretary to the counselors for over forty years. She loved her work and continues to remain active in her church choir. Quite amazing, yes.

Myrtle (Johnson) Collins

My sister Myrtle would follow her three older siblings out into the world, starting her own family. Myrtle would marry Rev J. C. Collins, who was a minister. She had five children: Carolyn, Standley, LaVera, Maxine, and Daryl Collins. Myrtle would continue the long legacy of work in the Baptist Church.

Myrtle is still a beautiful woman of 80 years of age. She is a hard working woman, full of faith and commitment to her family. I cannot count the number of grandchildren and great-grandchildren that she has. Myrtle, a trusted woman of faith and fairness, would work in the Baptist Church tirelessly, and would devote time to the younger children of the church. She also supervised the care of our mother during her illness. She never tired in her care during those days of illness that our mother would endure.

I must say, Martha and Cornelius's children have walked in the grace and mercy of a living God. Those seeds that were planted over a hundred years ago have come into their own, bearing fruits of service to one's church and community.

My siblings are aging very gracefully. They possess untold energy. They are beautiful women, who are full of wisdom and are still women who are beautiful to look upon. They do their own shopping, driving, and are still active in the community.

Chapter 7

-•◦◦❃◦◦•-

Cortez Carroll and the Carroll Family

Fear thou not; for I am with thee: be not dismayed; for
I am thy God:
I will strengthen thee; yea, I will help thee;
yea, I will uphold thee with the right hand of my
righteousness

Isaiah 41:10

My father, Cortez Carroll

After delivering her fourth child, my mother, Victoria, would start life again, making the best out of her circumstances in life. She eventually met my father, Cortez Carroll, who was from El Dorado, Arkansas. A handsome, six-foot country man with copper skin who wanted her and her four children. They would marry and would have six children together.

My father, Cortez Son Carroll [Cottesie (Sun)] Carroll

According to the U. S. Department of Commerce, Bureau of the Census of 1910, my father, Cortez Carroll, was born in 1906 in El Dorado, Arkansas. Cortez was born to John and Rose Carroll in Union County. They were married on December 25, 1889. John was 21 and Rosa, 18 (Arkansas County Marriage Index, 1837-1957). My father, Cortez, was one of 17 children. Oral history says that Cortez was one of 27 children. Seventeen were credited to my grandmother Rose. Some of their children would pass at birth. I am not sure of the exact number.

My paternal grandparents, John and Rose Carroll

FORM BC-655
FORMERLY FL 12-621
(5-14-65)

U.S. DEPARTMENT OF COMMERCE
BUREAU OF THE CENSUS
WASHINGTON, D.C. 20233

ns 957-130

Re: April 27, 1966

Cottesie Carroll
Route 6, Box 311
El Dorado, Ark.

Social Security Adm.
P.O. Box 1838
El Dorado, Ark. 71731

429-22-1343

The following information, including spelling of name, relationship, age, etc., is an EXACT COPY of the census record as reported by the census taker on the original schedule.

Census of 1910, taken as of April 15

Garner township

County ....Union........ State ....Arkansas........

Name	Relationship	Age	Place of birth	Citizenship
Garroll, John	Head			
" Rose	Wife			
" Rinda	Daughter			
" Francis	Daughter			
" Richard	Son			
" Ollie	Daughter			
" Charlie	Son			
" Will	Son			
" Marion	Son			
" Georgia	Daughter			
" *Cortez	Son	4	Arkansas	
" Lenard	Son			
" Rhee	Daughter			

*As reported to the Census Bureau

A. Ross Eckler
A. ROSS ECKLER
DIRECTOR
Bureau of the Census

The above information is furnished upon application with the understanding that in no case shall the information furnished be used to the detriment of the person or persons to whom the information relates, in accordance with Title 13, United States Code, Section 8.

The Bureau of the Census does not issue birth certificates, but this record is often accepted in place of one.

* U.S. GOVERNMENT PRINTING OFFICE : 1966 O—799-949

US Dept of Commerce document: The Carroll family

According to the oral history, which was passed on to me from my dad and his siblings, my grandmother Rose was of Creek origin, of the Native Americans of the new world. Aunt Georgia (Raburn), one of my father's sisters, would send me a picture of grandfather John and Rose Carroll. My grandmother was of a dark hue, with straight black hair, known to be Creek Indian.

Our paternal grandfather, John Carroll, was of a very light hue with a very long turned up mustache. A photograph of John and Rose will support that they were of native American ancestry. They were a very handsome couple, and would leave a wide spectrum of children. Colors that would vary from a light, copper color to a dark hue.

My father, Cortez, was a very rugged man to some degree and very rural. He loved the outdoors. He loved hunting, playing his harmonica, and sharing stories of his adventures and beliefs. I recall my dad going into the woods quite frequently hunting for squirrels, rabbits, and birds, which was part of our daily diet. He would strap his old brown cloth satchel over his shoulder, to carry his kill for the day. As a child, it was the height of our day, seeing my father pull the skin off a rabbit or squirrel or picking the feathers from black birds. I often felt sadden by the slaughter of animals. Most of our diet consisted of beans, navy beans, pinto beans, black eye peas, and lima beans. These staples, were mixed with rice, oat meal, mush from meal, spaghetti on special occasion, plenty of garden grown veggies and lots of rabbit and squirrel meat.

I can envision my dad, which I do often. He stood about 6'2" tall. He was of a copper hue with chiseled facial features, wide shoulders, a broad waist and hips. He always wore his hair in a combed back style, sometimes with a portion protruding to the front, truly bearing the stout features of Native American and African American heritage. Having studied the history of the Native Americans, as well as African Americans, and Europeans, I understand our history, as to who we are and where we originated.

My father's family started out as sharecroppers. Much later, their offspring would own the land out Mount Holly Road, in El Dorado, Arkansas. Like many African Americans and native people of that era, my father worked on the farm with very little formal education.

John and Rose Carroll were hard working individuals who worked hard to take care of their many children. They were of the Christian faith, and were an asset to their community. Oral history tells us, that when Grandpa John Carroll became ill in old age Grandmother Rose would send for the other woman that our grandfather had children with. They both would share in the care of our grandfather. We were told that the relationship worked out beautifully. As the father of twenty-seven children, John Carroll was an admired man, and would leave a large legacy to carry on his name.

During the Carroll Family Reunions, I was privileged to meet many of those beautiful offspring. As I write this history, the Carroll's have been located all over the United States, especially in Arkansas, Kansas City, Kansas, and Kansas City, Missouri. I have made an effort to remain in contact with as many family members, as I could throughout the years.

My father's obituary in 1972 listed the following siblings and children of John and Rose Carroll. His oldest sister, Rinda, was already deceased.

Sisters:

Georgia (Raburn), Los Angeles, California
Marie "Rhea" (Sanders), El Dorado, Arkansas
Bertha (Cook) Kansas City, Kansas
Tempie (Sanders), Phoenix, Arizona
Ollie (Smith), Los Angeles, California
Ruby (Smith), Los Angeles, California

Brothers:
Richard Carroll, Magnolia, Arkansas
Will Carroll, Kansas City, Kansas
Lenord Carroll, Kansas City, Kansas
Cecil Carroll, Kansas City, Kansas
Timothy Carroll, Gary, Indiana
Marion Carroll, Los Angeles, California
Jim Carroll, Los Angeles, California

I would have the privilege of meeting some of my father's siblings but I have been unable to obtain any information on many of them. I know that they were wonderful people, who lived and who left a mark in this earth.

Rinda Carroll

Rinda would be the first born; a beautiful daughter. Aunt Rinda, had a son named Albert who lived in Los Angeles, California. I don't know of any other children. I would get to know Albert. Albert would live to a wonderful age of 96. We would speak often on the telephone. Albert often talked of his mother, being the oldest and the first to leave the family home and to strengthen the way for the other siblings.

Through the years, I've witnessed the homegoing of many of the elders of the Carroll Clan. I have experienced the death of my father Cortez, and all of his sisters, Aunt Georgia, Aunt Bertha, Aunt Marie and Aunt Tempi, the youngest sister - all have passed away, Uncle Timothy, Uncle Bill, and Uncle Cecil have all left the family. Death is something that affects all of us. Being the natural process of life. We have not yet been able to escape its sting and its power over our lives. I wish I could have known my grandparents.

Chapter 8

Victoria and Cortez –
The Marriage, Family Life, and Struggles

He that dwelleth in the secret place of the most High
shall abide under the shadow of the Almighty.
I will say of the Lord, He is my refuge and my fortress:
my God; in him will I trust.

Psalm 91:1-2

The Marriage

Life could not have been easy, but quite complicated with ten children in the home. Trying to raise their family would create many challenges for them both. Cortez began to drink and was in a constant search for the right job to help support the family. Two individuals facing struggles of their own, and the issues that they both tried to overcome. Our parents' relationship was always one of challenges and discord. Their relationship would remain challenging throughout their years together. Growing up in a large family, we encountered many things, some pleasant, and others not so pleasant. Every experience would prepare me for future events in life.

My father would truly try to find work. I remember my father would rise early in the morning before daybreak. He would leave home before dawn every morning and would not return home until late evening. Often, we would have already gone to bed. I recall this was his habitual search for work. He often told my mother that everywhere he went, he would face the same response. "We are not hiring today." I remember that he was always "a day late and a dime short" as the old saying goes. I observed this routine most of my young life.

My father's constant inability to find work would be the catalyst that would cause the friction in our home. At times he would find what he would call piece work; work that was temporary, such as tearing down a building or erecting a building. This inconsistency would steer my dad to start his own small business, yard work. He did not own a vehicle, therefore his bicycle became his mode of transportation which limited how far he was able to travel, with all of his yard equipment in tow.

Together, my parents were not able to conquer the situations that they both found themselves in due to little education, poverty, lack of employment, and racism- all combined. We loved our father dearly. We loved them both, but we were surrounded by the influence of poverty, constant bickering over money, bills, alcohol, and violence. We wanted them to remain together, and they tried very hard to do so. However, their efforts were not enough for them to remain together. They would never divorce, but my father would retreat to his home town of Eldorado, Arkansas. After they separated from each other, my parents developed a more cordial relationship.

Their separation would make my mother's life more challenging. There would be consequences that trickled down throughout the family. My father's absence would cause my mother to work constantly, maintaining two jobs most of her working life.

In 1966, while I was in college at Arkansas AM&N College, I often went to spend weekends with my father in El Dorado on the property where he lived near his sister, and her children and grandchildren. I recall the beautiful, country atmosphere. At that time, my father had a small cottage on the land, near his sister, and the rest of the clan. I often went fishing in the lake near the home grounds. He had a quiet, peaceful life, after returning to his home-town. We children had love, respect, passion, and understanding, for our dad. Throughout this writing, I have reflected back to him often. He has left such an impact on my life. I want say that he was ordinary, but quite different in his own way.

Often when I went down on weekends, he would be lying in his homemade hammock under the tree. My mother would go and visit him often, as well as my sisters and brothers. My father never stopped providing for his children. It was a joy for me to see my dad at peace and finally enjoying his senior years, being surrounded by laughter, peace and children. We wanted him home around us of course. As children, we loved both of our parents. Experiencing the challenging relationship that they had would definitely affect us as children in some way. I believed they loved each other; how-ever there would be many factors that would contribute to their not being able to remain together.

Our father was never one who pursued the opposite sex. He seemed to have made his life as quiet and carefree as possible. Our mother often told us that our dad was never a womanizer and that she never had any problems with him being unfaithful to her. Their differences were more the result of the constant joblessness and his affair with alcohol. These were the factors of the conflict in their relationship.

Our dad would remain active and in fair health. He would discon-tinue his affair with alcohol and began attending church regularly. After retirement, he would develop arthritis, and what he called lumbago. He often told us that he was unable to ride in a vehicle, because of motion sickness and other conditions that had occurred.

I later realized the times in which they lived were designed to continue the plan of destruction of the Black family - designed to destroy all their dreams, and aspirations. I now understand the systems in place, hundreds of years hence, as well as today. They were in place to control the plight of the Black family, and future generations of their offspring.

Some Black men, including many of my father's friends, had jobs; however, more did not. These kinds of defeating situations would destroy, and did destroy, many Black families. Our family would be no exception to the rule. I had several childhood friends whose fathers were jobless and alcoholics.

I recall one very dear girlfriend, her family cooked outside. There were several children in the family. Both mother and father were alcoholics. Their lives were a complete shamble. If my mother had not had the faith and persistence that she held, our lives would have been a shamble as well.

My mother never gave up on the family. We were never homeless or without food and clothing. My mother possessed supernatural skills and abilities. She made most of our clothing, and prepared wonderful meals. We had large vegetable gardens in the summer. We worked the garden in the summer, and canned late summer and early fall. She often canned jellies, fruits, and veggies. Our mother always kept a freezer filled with food for the winter. Our pantry was always filled with beans, meal, rice, flour, peanut butter, powdered milk, butter, beef and spam in the can, and powered eggs. These staples were provided for families, who needed them. Many of my friend's received these free staples. They were called commodities and were handed out to needy families by the government. The commodities would feed many families, both Black and White. I must add, the food was very good. During those days, families were not given monetary assistance. However, the food kept lots of families from going hungry. Were we poor? Yes, we were very poor. I guess we did not realize that we were because most of our friends were in the same situation.

While growing up, I don't recall deer meat or lamb meat. I remember chicken because my family raised chickens. My grandmother, who lived with us during this time, had the role of preparing the chicken for the dinner table. She would pick the best one from the litter and ring his neck, which was a very sad sight to witness. My grandmother would grab an unsuspecting chicken and ring his neck and chop it off. A little cruel I thought, as a child. However, the thought of fried chicken in the afternoon made it less cruel. Fried chicken was always a delicacy at our home.

We always had lots of eggs which we collected daily from our little chicken house. We always enjoyed watching the chicken go into their chicken coops in late evening, and rising early at day break. Hearing our rooster crowing before day was a beautiful and expected sound each morning, to my young impressionable ears.

Our family also ate lots of chitterlings, neck bones, calf liver and the likes. Today, I do not eat pork. As a child, these meats were part of our diet. These were the foods that were readily available to us as we were growing up. Although I don't recall eating too many salads in those days, there were plenty of garden vegetables and lots of fruit. Life was very simple during those days.

Church Life

Another very important aspect of our lives was church. The Black Church is where we learned to speak and sing in front of an audience, and also how to praise God with fear and reverence of Him. We would miss the mark many times in trying to live for Him. However, we knew that to honor Him and live for Him was meaningful, in the now and the hereafter.

Our family attended Centennial Baptist Church in Pine Bluff, Arkansas under the leadership of Rev. S. B. Scott. The building was a beautiful brick structure, built by Blacks. It is still standing today. It has had several facelifts through the years, but it still represents so many memories. In later years the name would be changed to Indiana Street Baptist Church, Perhaps, because of the location on Indiana Street.

Dr. Lacy K. Solomon would take the reins after the death of Rev. Scott. I would be under the leadership of both pastors. I recall Rev. Scott being a giant of a preacher. A man who preached the word, without mixing it with things other than the bible.

It was mandatory to attend 9:30 a. m. Sunday School, followed by 11:00 a. m. service, returning at 6:00 p. m. for BTU (Baptist Training Union) and remaining for the 7:30 Sunday night preaching service. This was our Sunday worship schedule. No excuse could keep us from these services.

Requirements were not only to attend church, but to work in the church. The work of the church was to participate in the musical departments which required singing in the children's choir and giving speeches on special holidays (such as Christmas and Easter). It also included teaching Sunday School classes, ushering in the sanctuary, and reviewing the Sunday School lesson. No excuse could be given as to why you were unable to do it or could not perform the task. It was required.

Did we benefit from these teachings and meetings? I would say that we did. Looking back, I am most grateful for the solid foundation provided me and my siblings during those formative years. The challenges would provide me with strength, courage, faith and other characteristics - valuable lessons that have guided my life, providing me with survival skills and love of God and humanity.

The Carroll Children

Victoria and Cortez would have six children together. They were Manuel Leroy, Vernett, Ellis, Nadine, Vivian, and Alfred.

Manuel Leroy Carroll

My brother Leroy, my mother's fifth child and her first with my father, Cortez, had lots of energy, as do most males. His peers and classmates gave him the nickname "Slayer." Leroy was very tall in stature, over six feet. He was handsome with a reddish complexion. Leroy was a no-nonsense type of individual. He walked very tall and forcefully. You knew you were in the presence of a person who was going places.

Even as a youth, during his early life, Leroy depicted that he was on a mission, and that he had some place to be. While in high school, he would kill a fox. I don't know where he found a fox to shoot. Leroy turned this fox over to the Science Department of our High School, Southeast High. Dr. Gillard, our high school teacher, would prepare the fox for permanent exhibit in the class lab. This would be the beginning of his classmates calling him "Slayer" and a prelude of his life.

This one event would be a clue to what direction Leroy would take. Leroy always had a sense of courage and a defiant spirit. From my earliest memory of him, he operated outside of the norm. He often played childhood pranks on his siblings. This was his way of demonstrating he was in charge, and letting us know that he was present at all time.

I remember Leroy getting atop the refrigerator. This shocked my mother but not us, his siblings. On another occasion, he dyed his sandy hair a different color. His hair matched the chestnut color of his complexion. He never liked his natural color of hair and complexion.

As I look back over our youth, we often teased each other in many unkind ways. I believe some of the words spoken to each other left scars within the family. I now understand that many children in their earlier years of life, make many mistakes, missing the mark so often while experiencing feelings of loneliness, of being unloved and being misunderstood.

Hard work was mandatory in the family. Our mother always encouraged her children to work. We often followed Leroy to the cotton fields, chopping and picking cotton. The cotton fields were hard work, that paid very little. Working all day from sun up to sun down we were paid wages of three to four dollars for eight to twelve hours in the fields. LeRoy also worked at small jobs like most teenagers today. I recalled he worked at a shoe shop downtown, shining shoes, and he loved fishing.

LeRoy and my mother did not have the best relationship. I never understood why. I must admit he lived with a defiant and courageous spirit. As I've gotten older, I do understand that was the spirit of leadership.

When reaching the age of eighteen, LeRoy signed up for the United States Marine Corps. Our parents had no knowledge that he would join the military. He would move to Fort Wayne, Indiana, and live with our eldest sister, Dorlean Curry. It was there he made up his mind that he would join the Marine Corps. After joining, he changed his name to Manuel LeRoy Carroll instead of LeRoy Manuel Carroll which was his birth name.

Manual LeRoy Carroll

After joining the Marines, my brother would serve two tours of duty in Vietnam. During his second tour, LeRoy stepped on a land mine in GuanTri, Vietnam, which would mangle both legs. He was flown back to the United States. My mother and I were flown to Fort Sam Houston to see him. I was able to see and talk with LeRoy. He was in such grave pain and condition of his body. His injuries were of such, he was unable to survive. He would succumb to his injuries at 21 years of age.

I was a freshman at Arkansas AM&N College when this happened in 1966. I immediately dropped out of school. I was unable to carry on. The loss and pain was too great for me. I loved my brother dearly. I always wrote to him in Vietnam, and have letters fifty some years after his death. This would be one of the greatest losses in our family. He was our hero; a strong warrior. The family has held on to the memory or our beloved brother, Manuel LeRoy Carroll.

Following LeRoy's death in QuanTri, Vietnam, in 1966, our hometown of Pine Bluff, Arkansas would honor him by bestowing his name upon the VFW Building (Veterans of Foreign Wars). He was the first African American to receive such an honor in Pine Bluff; one that my brother very much deserved. He gave his life for his country, along with 58,000 other young Americans, fighting on foreign soil. His memory will always live in my heart. I think of him often and will always remember my brother, Manuel LeRoy.

Our first family reunion would be hosted in the VFW facility. The facility that bore his name in Pine Bluff, Arkansas. The Lamb, Johnson, and Carroll Reunion would bring together our family members from every part of the country. Fanily would attend from Washington, Indiana, Atlanta, Los Angeles, Philadelphia, Ohio, Texas, and yes, Arkansas. The main focus of our reunion was to honor our fallen brother, Leroy, to celebrate his legacy, and to celebrate our oldest brother, Wallace Johnson.

LeRoy did marry before going into his second tour of duty in Vietnam. The whereabouts of his wife have remained a mystery for over fifty years. After the burial of our brother, this individual disappeared. There were no children to this union. While living in Los Angeles, California, I had a brief encounter with her. Her name at that time was Lillie Jean Carroll. She was born in Little Rock, Arkansas. We have tried to locate her, but to no avail. This was a part of LeRoy's life that has remained a mystery to his family. A mystery that would remain unclear to us. We have had to release it to the universe. Only God knows what actually happened. A beautiful, young, courageous life gone too soon.

Vernett Morning Star Kittrell

Sibling number six, Vernett, attended Arkansas AM&N College. She would marry Fred Kittrell from New York City at the age of 18 in the living room of the family home. They moved to Philadelphia where she became a licensed cosmetologist. As of this writing, Vernett is 72 years of age. She is very active, very creative, and very spiritual as an Indian Shaman. She has carved out a beautiful and creative life for herself and family. Vernett's children are Frednando, Orlando, Andria, and Juan Dakota.

Vernett has five grandchildren: Rosa, Lydiah, Nahdia, Fredando Ali, and Dyonesia Victoria all of whom are Frednando's children. They continue to live in New York and Philadelphia, and are doing quite well. I have never gone to Philadelphia to visit, however it is on my bucket list, along with other places and family members to visit.

Ellis Eugene Carroll

Ellis was sibling number eight. While growing up, we called Ellis 'Genie'. This was the name that we would call him, all of his life. Genie seemed quite fitting for him. He would leave home at the age of eighteen.

Ellis was quite handsome, and had a very eye-catching swagger about himself. He would marry Brenda Whitmore. He was the father of eight children: Ellis Jr., Tara, Britany, Roderick, Marcus, Brandon, DeCarlos, and Johnathan.

Ellis Eugene Carroll

Genie, as we called him, would never talk back to our mother as some of her children would do. Whenever she would lecture him, as she did often, he would never try to explain himself or refute her - as she called "talking back." Genie would maintain a quiet and easy persona at all times. Genie would either smile, or just walk away. Our mother credited Ellis as being able to clean the kitchen better than any of her children.

Ellis would work for the Cotton Belt Rail Road for several years. He was very active in the community and would work with voter registration efforts. He was known for his gift of singing gospel music. He became a member of a local gospel group called the Gospel Pioneers and remained a part of this group for many years. Ellis also acted in local plays in Pine Bluff and even in Little Rock, Arkansas.

Ellis was impeccable in his dress, and had a strong sense of order and style, so it was no surprise when he was called into the fashion world to model on many occasions. Ellis would maintain his boyhood weight throughout his adult life.

During his younger years, Ellis participated in the Civil Rights Movement in Pine Bluff. He was one of the first African American students to integrate the local segregated Pine Bluff High School. He was a person who was very quiet and direct.

Ellis would pass on at 63 years of age, leaving us quietly and unexpected, just as he lived his life; leaving a void in the family. He has truly been missed. Ellis was one of a kind, having many friends, people who loved him dearly. His going home celebration was truly a celebration of life. Indiana Street Baptist Church, our home church, was filled to capacity with people who cared for our beloved Genie. His son, Ellis, Jr., would precede him in death, having been killed by an unknown shooter while walking home in Pine Bluff, Arkansas.

Nadine Carroll Hayes

Our youngest sister, Nadine (number nine) would marry at seventeen years of age, right after high school, to Verne Hayes, in Pine Bluff, Arkansas - a beautiful young couple, heading for the Marine Corps. They would spend 20 years in the United States Marine Corps. To that union two children, Ahmad B. Hayes, and Stormie Hayes Turner, were born. They have one grandson, Jacob Seth Turner.

Their military life would be very rewarding for them. Verne would retire from the military, making their home in Dallas, Texas. Nadine would return to college, getting a B.S. Degree, and later a Master's Degree from Dallas Theological Seminary and a degree in Psychology, following the call of God on her life, as a licensed minister.

Nadine has worked in the Dallas School District for many years, and has been very involved in her community and the work of

Ministry. Nadine, being the youngest girl in the family, worked in the church growing up, and was also one of the first African Americans to integrate Pine Bluff High School in our town where she would play in the Pine Bluff marching band. A beautiful and no nonsense woman of character and creativity, Nadine is currently living in Dallas, Texas in full time ministry of the Gospel of Jesus Christ. She continues to be a leader, living a purpose-filled life having been baptized by the legendary Bishop, T. D. Jakes while serving in his ministry.

Alfred Dewayne Carroll

Alfred, sibling number ten, is the youngest of the family; Victoria and Cortez's youngest child. I recall my mother walking to and from work. The family did not own a vehicle at that time. My mother dressed to disguise her tenth pregnancy. She wore a black skirt and a large white blouse. We as children had no idea that our mother was pregnant with her tenth child. By this time, there were five children in the home. Our mother would go to work as usually. She would continue the routine of rearing the five of us who were still home.

She would bear no appearance of being with child. How could she have kept this pregnancy concealed from us. I ponder to this day. I remember our mother coming home from work, and requesting newspapers. She would go into her room and close the door. We assumed she would be taking a nap from her long day of work, and walking home from work. I recalled a woman coming to the home that we knew was a nurse. We had seen her at the clinics during our visits to the health center.

This Black woman in a beautiful white uniform was Mrs. Pridgette, an African-American midwife. She had worked under my grandmother, who was a retired midwife, years earlier. We began to suspect that our mother was ill, but there were no words or information given us. We did not hear a cry or any sounds that indicated that life was coming into the world. At the end of this visitation, we were called into my mother's bed room, and she would introduce our new brother to us. We were confounded, at the least.

It is important to note that children did not ask questions about family business. I must have been about ten or eleven years of age. Our parents did not involve us in their business, nor did they explain things to us. Perhaps they should have, however, there was a line that children did not cross with adults. We were not allowed to listen in on our parents conversations and discuss their conversations. We had a reverence for our parents. We had an understanding that our parents were not to be questioned but respected and honored. This would be the norm in child rearing for many of the Black families that I know, or that lived in our neighborhood.

There was a code of conduct regarding parents. Many of us believed that we were to honor and respect our parents, just as the Bible had said. We did not want to disrespect our parents, just as we did not want to disrespect our God.

As of this writing, Alfred and his wife, Sharon, are the parents and stepparents of five beautiful children: Alinderia, Alfred Jr., Candis, Courtney, and David. Alfred is also a grandfather of two children. After completing college at UAPB. Alfred would get his Master's Degree and PhD in Education. He is very involved in the church and the community, becoming a Justice of the Peace, school teacher and elementary principal in the Pine Bluff School District.

Our mother always had high expectations for her last and tenth child. She would inform the family that her last child would answer the call of the ministry. She said that he would preach the gospel of Jesus Christ one day. Victoria had prophesied correctly about her tenth child. Alfred would become a deacon in his church and is currently preaching the Gospel of Jesus Christ. I'm sure our mother is looking down and smiling.

Myrtle Collins <u>Left to Right</u>: Wallace Johnson, Vivian A. Carroll Jones, Doris Duncan, Nadine Hayes, Vernett Morning Star Kittrell, Rev. Alfred Carroll. <u>Insert</u>: Darlean Johnson Curry

Chapter 9

The Seventh Child - Vivian A. Carroll Jones

"The Word of the Lord came to me saying. Before I formed you in the womb, I knew you, Before you were born I set you apart."

Jeremiah 1:4

H aving introduced my siblings as best as I could, I now want to discuss my life.

I am the seventh of ten children. My mother often spoke of me being her seventh child. She would mention to her friends and family that I was child number seven, and that I was quite different from her other children. I never understood if she meant this in a good way or a negative way. I was never treated special or felt special – as a matter of fact, I would feel just the opposite among my siblings and around my mother. I was probably punished a little bit more than the rest.

Being the seventh of ten children, I was constantly being acknowledged as her seventh child. I did not understand her meaning, nor did I ever ask her to explain it to me. I sensed that my mother knew that I was different and was treated as such. I was not treated in a special way, but in a different way.

God's Call

At a very early age, I would sense the call of God on my life. As a result of His call, I would begin a quest to find out how I fit into the scheme of God's plan for my life. I sought his presence, and His leading. I looked for Him in the day time. I searched the skies for Him. I would lie on the ground and search the heavens for Him. I would lie in bed at night and look for His appearing and His coming. At a very early age I knew of Him and His presence in the earth. I labored hard to understand things, and sought to be honest in my communication and behavior. However, I did not measure up at all times. I sensed that I had a glimpse into the spirit realm.

One Sunday morning, while preparing for Sunday School, I would hear my name called. At that time, there were six children in the home. Four of my nine siblings had already left the home having married and starting their own families.

My mother and I were running late for Sunday School. Several of my siblings had left for church earlier. I was late because I hadn't gotten my clothes ready the night before, which was always mandatory. Clothes pressed, hair done, shoes polished was the normal routine. My mother even prepared Sunday's meal on Saturday evening for Sunday.

My mother and our lagging behind was not the norm. As I rushed to prepare for Church, I heard my name – Ann. The call was very clear and soft. I thought my mother had called me. I rushed to her, and asked if she had called. She replied no. I continued to dress for Sunday School. Once again, I heard this voice call my name. Again, I promptly went to my mother. My mother replied, "Get ready for Church!" By now, my mother had raised her voice, and began to scold me. Surely I was not imagining that my name was being called. This had never happened before.

I would hear this call a third time. Just as before, I ran to my mother for the third time. By now, she was very upset. Her reply being the same, *"Let's get to Church!"* As I walked away from her, I said, *"It must be God calling me."* From that day forward, I felt that the Creator had called. I maintained that belief as I moved forward in my life. I knew, something special and unusual had occurred that Sunday Morning, as I was getting ready for Sunday School.

I recall the days of revival, sitting on the mourner's bench, while being encouraged to give our lives to Jesus Christ, and denounce the world, and the works of satan. I made a decision to live for Jesus. After denouncing satan and asking forgiveness of all my sins, I would be baptized at 12 years of age under the leadership of Reverend Scott.

As a child and young adult, I knew God to be real. I would often lie awake at night, believing that He would appear to me. I recall a voice calling my name when no one else was around. I immediately felt, it was the voice of God, calling me to Himself. From an very early age, I held in my heart that He had called me. I never wavered from that knowledge of being called. Even today, at 70 years of age, I nurture and honor that call I heard.

I continue my search for His presence, and His voice. I have not heard that audible voice since childhood, but I can say beyond any doubt in my mind, that I had heard the still, quiet voice of God. I have never attempted to reason it away. It is settled in my mind for eternity.

My life continues to be a life of hunger and pursuit of the spiritual and the unknown relating to the Creator and His creation. My endless search for God has led me to search for Him in the quietness, in the storms, and in dreams, seeking to know Him.

My search for God would leave me with lots of questions about the known and the unknown. Throughout my early life and even today as an adult, I am still searching for answers to the mysteries of life. My searching has led me into churches, schools, studying the bible, and other extensive works and books.

Was I a good child who never made mistakes? Quite the contrary! Perhaps that is the reason God was calling me in a voice that I could hear Him. Throughout my journey, I would miss the mark often - getting into lots of mischief, making wrong decisions, meeting the wrong people and doing the wrong things. Now I understand the call that I would hear as a child.

<u>My childhood</u>

I would be known by my friends and family as being very odd and peculiar. I guess you could say these character traits would follow me throughout my life - being misunderstood, insecure, ashamed, a stutterer, fearful, and alone.

Early in life, I discovered that I was a chronic stutterer. This defect in my speech would make my life very difficult. I was often ridiculed by my peers, and wanted to communicate as little as possible. This handicap would follow me on into adult life. The fear of speaking would hold me captive for many years.

A wonderful English teacher, Mrs. Charolette Standfield, told me that my stuttering was caused by nervousness and fear, and that I could overcome it. She told me to speak slowly and to take a deep breath before speaking. Along with prayer, and getting over the fear, my speech began to improve. Today, I am not afraid to speak. I have learned to face my fears. *"For God has not given us a spirit of fear, but of power ,and of love and of a sound mind."* (2 Timothy 1:7) God has given me the grace to face the fear, and to speak in front of large audiences. I am finally free and for that I am thankful.

As I got older, I would eventually master more of these flaws by seeking the intervention of the Creator into my life to help me. The transformation did not happen overnight. The transformation would come after many years of struggle and embarrassing moments; many trials and error, and the grace of God.

My work ethic was developed very early in life. During my youth and adolescence, as early as eight or nine years of age, I had responsibilities not only within the home, but babysitting the neighborhood children. I recall several neighborhood families that I had the responsibility of watching their children.

My friends and I would go throughout our neighborhood collecting soda bottles to resell back to the Coke company. We would receive two cents for each clean bottle that we returned to them. The two cents would add up. I recall that my girlfriend and I collected a large tub of bottles. We made enough to put a skirt and sweater on layaway. It would take weeks to pay out the layaway.

During those years, I sold greeting cards and religious plaques to neighbors. Many years later as I got older, my entrepreneurship skills and spirit would surface. I ventured into selling Avon products, Stanley products, and Amway. I would have yard sales with books, antiques, jewelry, and clothes. I had a strong desire to sell and to build a business. This desire would follow me on into my adult life.

> *Call unto me, and I will answer thee, and show thee great and mighty things, which thou knowest not.*

> Jeremiah 33:3

A Wife, Mother and Grandmother

I would meet my future husband, Charles Jones, while a teenager. My mother loved him believing he would be a good husband for me. Prior to marriage Charles was drafted into the Army. My mother would ward off any other prospective beaus.

After Charles returned to Pine Bluff, it was felt that marriage would soon follow –but it did not. So it was, at the age of 20, my 10-month old daughter, Chrystal, and I would travel to Los Angeles, California to begin a new life. Amazingly, I had no apprehension about traveling at 20 years of age with a young baby.

Charles would follow six months later and we would marry in the Los Angeles County Courthouse. We would live in Los Angeles for about three years. During this time our other two children, twins Omarr and Danyelle, would be born. Although our stay in California would be brief, it would be a wonderful time; but home was calling us to return to Arkansas, which I have never regretted. Charles never wanted to raise our family in California. We both agreed that Arkansas would be a much better place to watch our children grow up.

I must say Charles was always a good provider. He would prove to be a strong provider with a diligent work ethic. He was very detailed about many things and would make the best decisions possible for the family. He had many qualities that would prove to be the best for our family. Our children would demonstrate those qualities in their own lives, working hard and never giving up until the job was done.

I can say Charles would always put his family first. We did not agree on many things; however, through the years we were able to combine our parenting skills for the good of the family to accomplish the desired outcome.

Charles graduated from Arkansas AM&N (now the University of Arkansas at Pine Bluff / UAPB) with a degree in Mechanical Engineering. He would insist that the children remain at home and attend UAPB, even though they received scholarships to out-of-state colleges. We agreed that if the children remained home and lived at home they would be able to start out without debt. This would prove to be the best decision for the children because they maintained good grade point averages and graduated from UAPB without owing for student loans. I thank God that we were able to give our children the foundation needed to give them the best start in life that we could.

The University of Arkansas at Pine Bluff has proven to be such a gift to many students and families. Our oldest granddaughter, Asia Jones Colen, would become the latest graduate of this great institution.

Charles retired as a blacksmith, welder from the Cotton Belt and Union Pacific Railroad after 27 years. For several years he was an instructor at Arkansas AM&N College (now UAPB) in the Vocational Department. Charles continues to enhance, support, and strengthen his children's lives. Whether working in their offices, or tending to the grandchildren – always listening, encouraging, and pushing them forward.

The season of rearing my children was a beautiful season. I thank The Most High that I had the experience of marriage, the season of watching my children grow up and find their places in life, and raising their own children.

The Bible tells us that *"Children are a gift from God"* (Psalm 127:3 NASB). Even before I read these words in the scripture, I knew this in my heart. My children - Chrystal, Omarr, and Danyelle Jones, and my six beautiful grandchildren, (Asia Jones Colen, Ethan O. Walker, Victoria A. Walker, Dylan Jones, Peyton Jones and Bianic) have been wonderful gifts. They are one of the greatest gifts, and greatest blessings, that I have ever received. This wonderful blessing has enriched my life over and over.

L-R: Danyelle Walker, Victoria Walker, Ethan Walker, Ben Johnson, Chrystal Johnson, Vivian Jones, Charles Jones, Asia Colen Jones, Dani Jones, Omarr Jones, Payton Jones, Dylan Jones

I knew that I would have to nurture and guide this gift. I knew that I was entrusted with this gift for a higher purpose. How did I know? I now believe and know that the Creator, who is all knowing, knew that I would tell them about Him and his goodness and would do all that I could to teach them about their Creator and Maker. As a young mother of 20 years of age, I would set out on a course of action that would be a life-long venture of introducing our children to the Creator.

The plan of introduction would begin with Sunday School at a very early age. The children would learn to work in the Church as part of the call of the Gospel. They learned to give reverence and respect for the Church and its purpose in our lives and to participate in the church through the Children's Choir, ushering, speeches, and giving offerings. They would learn the importance of confession of one's faith in the teachings of Jesus Christ, and the responsibility and importance of aligning one's life with His teachings. As a result of their faith and acknowledgement to become followers of Christ, they would be baptized, as an action of their faith. I must say, with a smile, the three of them would be baptized on three separate occasions: being sprinkled by the Priest as infants; second, being baptized in the river during elementary school age, and their third baptism which would be in the Baptist Church during adolescent years. Would this have some influence on their lives? I'm sure that it would have some influence as to taking the teachings of Christ very serious.

The rearing of my children and the relationship to my grandchildren are closely related to how I was raised. I found myself being old fashioned and strict. I did eliminate some of the old ways, especially the rules and language that were not conducive to developing children and grandchildren with a healthy outlook about themselves. Many of our parents did not encourage the positive strengths in our lives growing up. Some of the negative behaviors that we demonstrated were met with physical punishment. This was their way of disciplining us. This type of punishment often created negative energy between parent and child.

Being one of ten children would tax my parents to a level that I would not have been able to endure. I can only imagine what it must have been like, to raise ten children and endure the hardship of racism and other challenges they would face. How many of our parents struggled in their daily lives rearing their children. I truly salute them, how they overcame the hardships they faced.

I must say that the lives of my own children, as adults in their mid-forties, are very reflective of their spiritual values and beliefs. They, too, have passed their Christian values and practices, spreading their wings and giving me beautiful grandchildren.

I am thankful that in their personal lives they have chosen to be productive individuals and servants of humanity. I can truly say that I have seen the goodness and the blessings of Our Creator. I have seen how His teachings and practices can guide you to a life of service and peace; not that of a religious individual, but that of a spiritual person led by the guidance of the Holy Spirit. As my children and grandchildren serve humanity and their God - I am most grateful and most blessed.

<u>Walks of Faith</u>

During the early years of raising my three children, I would seek part-time jobs in order to be available to my children especially while they were small. I answered an ad in the newspaper for a clerk typist to retype a work manual for the incoming supervisor. I felt this would be a great part-time job for me. The job was at a local bag plant in my hometown. The pay was great and I could perform some of the work at home.

I answered the job in the newspaper and even got an interview. The assignment would take about three to four months and would allow me to come in at various hours. I really wanted this assignment. I thought the interview went very well and this was the job for me. I really believed I would get it.

I called the company three days later to see if they had made a selection. I was regretfully told that I did not get the assignment and that someone else was selected. I must say I was quite disappointed. When the conversation ended, I promptly said aloud, "*If God wants me to have this job, they will call me back.*" I had peace about the outcome. Within a very short period of time, maybe two or three days later, I received a call from the company offering me the job - if I was still interested in it. I said, "*Yes, I am interested*" and accepted the job.

Even though I was not their first choice, I was so excited. I felt in my spirit I was supposed to have that job. The results I would say were a success for me and the company as well. It was a win-win situation. I would spend two hours in the office and the remaining work was done at my home.

The Mink Coat

I am the vine, ye are the branches: He that abideth in me, and I in him, the same bringeth forth much fruit: for without me ye can do nothing. [John 15:5]

In my early forties, I felt that I was old enough to wear a mink coat. I had always wanted a real mink and decided to run a classi-fied ad in the local newspaper in search of a pre-owned mink. I was willing to pay at least $50.00 for a used coat. I felt this was a fair amount to pay for a mink coat. The ad read: "Would like to purchase pre-owned mink." Within a few days, I received a call from a mature female voice. The caller had a mink coat to sell. When she told me her name and where she lived, I knew who she was.

The caller was a retired school teacher and her husband was a retired school principal. I was quite astounded. I was invited to come by and see the coat. I was truly excited. When I arrived they recognized who I was. I must say this lady had three mink coats. She encouraged me to try them on. This wonderful classy lady would sell me the most beautiful mahogany mink coat I had ever seen. She told me that she had purchased the coat in New York. I was so thankful to have such a beautiful mink coat. She finally asked me, *"How did you know that I had a mink coat to sell?"* I told her that I did not know. I just followed the leading of the Holy Spirit. The Creator knows everything. *'I will go before you and make the crooked places straight.'* Isaiah 45:2(a)

First home in Pine Bluff:

> *And my people shall dwell in a peaceable habita-*
> *tion, and in sure dwellings, and in quiet resting places.*
> [Isaiah 32:18]

After relocating from Los Angeles, California back home to Pine Bluff, Arkansas, we rented a home on East 6th street. This was a beautiful , white wooden frame home with beautiful hardwood floors, two large bedrooms and one bath. We were quite blessed to be able to rent this home. A beautiful well-kept home for a family with three small children. We would remain in this bungalow home for a little over a year. The only drawback was the home was on a main, busy street, which was not suitable for small children.

After adapting to the rental for several months, we wanted our own home and an ideal location for our children. Along with a friend, I visited a very nice area with attractive brick homes. Although we had decided not to buy immediately, my friend was ready to purchase. Her husband was a veteran, just as mine was. She found this beautiful grey brick home and we both were excited. Directly across the street was this wonderful antique brick home with green shutters and a green wooden door. With my first view, I knew this was the home for my family. My favorite color at the time was green, and it was a lovely avocado green.

My heart was set on this home. This area was very nice, and I had always wanted a brick home, and this would be a nice area to raise a family. I immediately told my husband about the property, and made an appointment to view the home. The process had begun. I could hardly contain the excitement.

Prior to moving, I would visit the home daily, routinely driving by to check on the property. We would now have three large bedrooms, a bath and a half, and a beautiful kitchen with lovely cabinets. I must also add the home had gorgeous green carpet and complimentary avocado appliances. We purchased this charming brick home for $19,000 dollars, with a monthly house payment of $169.00. The home is now paid for and is still very beautiful. Most of the old neighbors have passed on and a few are still there. This was truly a gift from the Creator, and a perfect place for my family. I marvel at the goodness of God.

Home in Little Rock, Arkansas

Life would change after the three children grew to adulthood and the addition of five grandchildren. Being single for well over 20 years now and living in an apartment, I desired a home of my own once again. I began to miss the privacy and the freedom to garden and watch things grow. Over the years I wanted my own home again. I had made several attempts to secure a loan to buy a home. I found myself not having the down payment, or a high enough credit score. Year after year, I would attempt to purchase a home.

Once again, I found myself trying to overcome hurdles, and using my faith in achieving what seemed to be impossible. I also learned that it doesn't get easier as you age, nor do doors automatically open up for you just because you are wiser. I often think of my parents and grandparents, and the times that they lived in. The challenges that they faced and overcame were much harder than what we face today. Therefore, I make every effort to change my thinking or feeling sorry for myself.

We would watch our mother struggle with ten children and little education. Her life was very difficult; mostly making ends meet, alone with very little assistance. My mother would not own her own home until eight of her children were grown and married. She would eventually purchase the rental property that most of us grew up in. The home was weather worn and in dire need of paint and a roof. Over the years, mother was able to do some home improvements. One of the oddities of the house was that the bathroom was on the back porch. However, it became our home.

I relocated to Little Rock in my very late forties - not a very good time in life to start over again, or maybe it was a wonderful time to start over again. Either way, I would take the plunge. I have never regretted my decision to start life over again. Another act of faith, I trusted God and I chose to start over again. After living in a nice apartment for sixteen years, I wanted to own my own home again.

Following many years of looking at homes, and getting disappointed, I would find a 60-year old, 1300 square foot brick little cottage, in an area that I did not think I would like. However the home and the area would prove to be a very nice neighborhood. Following much prayer, and stepping out in faith, I was able to find a bank that would make me a loan to purchase my home. Without any more delay, I started packing 30 days prior to my moving day.

My garden was established the first year that I moved in. I have been able to create a beautiful English Garden, planting numerous boxwoods, and junipers. In creating my garden I used lots of bags of brown mulch to hold the moisture in the ground around the trees and scrubs. In some areas, where the grass is limited, I have used pea gravel to create a warm eye tone. My garden also consists of seven and eight-feet spruce trees and lots of areas of monkey grass. My English garden has been visited by many who ask to view it, including many curious friends and neighbors.

As the garden evolved, I continued to add other features, including a beautiful Asian Garden. I used large boulders in my Asian Garden, but only the ones I could move on my own. I also included a small Chinese temple about four feet in height, made of solid concrete. My garden is quite beautiful and relaxing and something I am very proud of. There are some that have doubted that I planted and created this oasis. I call it an oasis because I spend many hours in my yard, and many hours establishing its' effect. Every bit of work was my creative vision that the Creator gave me. I would eventually be honored as having the yard of the month and received a monetary award. I felt very honored.

The address of my new home amazingly happens to be the number 34; the number seven being my favorite number - three and four equaling seven. I would move into my home the seventh month of the year and also the seventeenth day. Being child number seven in a family of ten children, I knew I had made the right decision, and that the Creator once again had provided for me. To God be the Glory, forever. As usual, I chose to follow my peace and my God-given instinct.

As of July 2018, I have lived in my home for nine and a half years. I have encountered some challenges, such as replacing the bathroom commode, replacing the bathroom vanity, and replacing kitchen and bathroom floors with beautiful tile. I waited seven years to put in granite counter tops in my galley kitchen. I painted the entire home myself, a new roof was added by a city grant, which would save me $5,000.00. This was truly a blessing.

Shortly after moving into the neighborhood, I was contacted by mail indicating that the City of Little Rock was involved in revitalizing the area I lived in. Since the University of Little Rock was in the vicinity, I assumed they had a project to invest some grant money into the area. The reason they were working in the area was not communicated to me. I moved in at the right time and in the right location. I have always wondered why they contacted me. I now understand why I was contacted and received such favor. The end result was a new roof for my home at no cost. It was all part of the plan of favor and the goodness of our Creator. Amen.

My sharing these special events is not to focus on the things that Our Father gives us - and yet He meets our daily needs. He provides the things that we need. My intention is to convey how life is never without challenges and hurdles to cross over. It is to share how things can seem impossible for man to realize how to navigate through them, but the Creator works them out for us. Ecclesiastes 9:11 - *The race is not to the swift or the strong...* is often coupled with Matthew 10:22 / Matthew 24:13 - *but he who endures to the end shall be saved.* We face disappointments, challenges, hurdles, the likes - we press on. Every good day that we experience is a day to rejoice and be thankful. Tomorrow will be different. *To God be the Glory*! Our perseverance, our faith, our willingness to not give up, and to do those things that are required of us, as well as our constant focus and energy will bring about the manifestation of the things we are believing for. Hebrews 11:6 *But without faith it is impossible to please Him. For he that cometh to God must believe that he is, and that He is a rewarder of them that diligently seek Him.* The Creator has hardwired us to press forward and not give up.

My Education

I can recall some early years of my life, attending Indiana Street School in Pine Bluff, Arkansas, then attending Southeast Jr. and Sr. High School. After high school, I attended Business School, and Nursing School, before going on to the University of Arkansas at Pine Bluff (UAPB). In 1983, at the age of 34, I received a B.S. in Social Studies at UAPB. Years later, at 53 years of age, I received a B. S. Degree from the University of Arkansas at Little Rock, Arkansas. By this time, I had fully established in my own mind that I had a love for learning and growing.

In my early 50's I attended Agape School of World Evangelism for two years. Having a strong sense and responsibility to share the good news of the Gospel, I wanted to study the teachings of Jesus, and His Life, and the transformation and power that it could have upon one's life.

Upon completion of Missionary and Bible School, I felt prepared to share the gospel of Jesus Christ with whomever I would meet in life. The Word of God, that I had discovered could transform one's life and give them a sense of hope and purpose. This Gospel has transformed many lives throughout the ages of history and empowers an individual when they get to know the One who spoke and lived, and learn to walk in the reality of its power.

The Fall Season of my Life

As I enter the fall of my own life, I realize how blessed I have been. I realize the importance of faith, family, and most importantly the recognition of the Creator in one's life. A life of prayer, hope and God enables one to see into the future, knowing that tomorrow will be better, brighter and yes, full of laughter. The believer is promised a better day. Regardless of how dark the moment may seem, tomorrow will be brighter, if we just don't give up or cave in. We move forward, taking one day at a time. Sometimes tears are in order. Sometimes good old rest works. Whatever it takes, we continue to move forward into our tomorrows, thanking God for each day and every step.

Psalm 23:1-3a; 6a reads "*The Lord is my Shepherd and I shall not want. He maketh me to lie down in green pastures. He leadeth me beside the still waters. He restoreth my soul... surely goodness and mercy shall follow me all the days of my life...*" How many times, I have had to quote these verses aloud and walk in it. These are the times He – God – has to make His children rest. There have been times I have needed long periods of rest in order to survive and to move forward. I thank God that He knows when our bodies have gone as far as they need to go. He is my Shepherd and He watches over me.

When I've rested, I feel stronger and revived. He releases me to start afresh, letting go of the past and looking to a bright new day. "God is our refuge and strength, a very present help in trouble" (Psalm 46:1) His ways are perfect and I trust Him, He is my all and all. "For *in the time of trouble, He will hide me in His pavilion.*" (Psalm 27:5). I have been hidden many times until the storm has passed. *To God be the Glory, for all that He has done.* There have been many times that He has delivered me *"from the snare of the fowler"* (Psalm 91:3). So many times He covered me with His feathers, and under His wings. I have trusted Him, many times escaping from the pit and the snares, some of my own making. Whatever the case, He delivered me in time. *To God be the Glory for His goodness and His mercy.*

Transitioning through life is not easy. We face many things and do many things as we try and unravel this puzzle that has been carefully hidden from our view. Life's lessons are clearly preparing us to navigate through life. Life's lessons can be wonderful teachers. The fires of life make us qualified individuals who have been tried and tested. This enables us to be a light to someone else or the next generation that's searching for meaning and purpose in life.

Often we do things that will surface later in life. If we had the chance to do it over again, would we? Could we? Ecclesiastes 12:1 states *"Remember now thy Creator in the days of thy youth, while the evil days come not, ..."* I've learned to seek the Creator early in dealing with life's situations. When we seek His path, we make fewer wrong and hurtful choices in life.

While traveling in this life, forgiving ourselves is very important. We have to let the past go, forgive ourselves and forgive others in order that we can be free and live the best life that we can. We must not live in condemnation. We are being shaped for the Master's use. I have learned to embrace my past. The past has prepared me for the future. My past has strengthened and molded me. The past has brought me to this junction in life. I would not be the person that I am today if I had not overcome the past - good, bad or indifferent. *God be Praised!* I am delivered, born again, forgiven, pruned, saved, set free, healed, redeemed, tested by fire, shaped on the anvil and now I am ready for the Master's use, seeking His guidance, grace, and mercy each day.

Looking back, I often wonder how we made it while providing care for our ailing mother for eighteen months and the loss of both parents. Our father would pass on suddenly in his home-town of El Dorado, Arkansas. We kept our faith in our God. We had good neighbors and friends. We had the church. We all had small jobs or worked in the cotton fields spending days chopping cotton, soy beans, and the like. Fieldwork taught us how to work and to save our money. We were taught to put our resources together for the good of the entire family. My mother was an expert in man-aging money.

My own life would take on many forms, overcoming challenges and hurdles as I journeyed through life. Now that I have seen some seventy years, I can understand the words of David the King of Israel when he said: *"I have been young, and now am old; yet have I not seen the righteous forsaken, nor his seed begging bread"* (Psalm 37:25). These words are so true. The Creator has kept us safe and protected and continues to guide us throughout this life as we daily acknowledge Him, seeking His wisdom and guidance, each day. *To God be the Glory forever and forever.* Amen.

I am most grateful that I have been allowed to experience and explore different areas of life. Most of my life has been spent pur-suing education, studying, and learning how to live a more produc-tive and spiritual life. I study the Holy Scripture and the history of African people prior to American and current history. My constant pursuit of spirituality, business adventures and self-improvement in every area of my life has led me to various jobs and meeting many types of individuals.

I am a very passionate individual harboring a disdain for injus-tices and man's inhumanity to his fellow man. Civil rights and social justice for all people, especially people of African descent, is extremely important to me. I have a desire to make a difference, wherever I can, for the uplifting of people of color. I want to make the world a better place as a result of my having been here. I thank the Creator for every opportunity, and pray that I will know the time of His visitation in my life (Luke 19:44).

Chapter 10

Storytelling and Old Sayings
Grandma Florence, My Mother
& My Father

Every word of God is pure:
he is a shield unto them that put their trust in him.

Proverbs 30:5

My Grandmother's Stories

Grandma always talked about the Ringling Brothers Circus. When she was a little Girl, the circus came to town. It would be a wonderful experience for her. She did not actually attend the circus, however all children knew that the circus was in town. She would observe all the large elephants and lions. To a small child this was quite exciting.

When I moved to Los Angeles, California in my early twenties, the Ringling Brother's Circus was performing in the Los Angeles Area. I would take my oldest daughter Chrystal to see the Ringling Brother's Circus. Throughout the performances, I thought of my dear grandmother Florence. As a young adult I was moved by the animal acts, the performances of the huge lions and elephants. I, too, would experience the cheers and the excitement of being present. The lights, the flying acts, the cheers of children, were such a treat for me.

Grandma said that many children of her day would run off to be with the circus. When the circus would leave town, it was discovered that children were missing from their homes. Even though there were no cases in point, if Grandma Florence said it - it was true of her day. Her words were always so powerful and filled with truth. That was how my grandmother lived her life. Grandmother Florence, being very close to the Creator, would never tarnish the name of her God with an untruth.

Grandma often talked about how cruel the war was and the fear that the Yankees brought to their community. She said during the Civil War, when the Yankee Soldiers came to town, her father would gather them inside. Saying very loudly, "You children better get inside!" She said the Yankee soldiers were known for raiding the homes of white families and grabbing their babies, and dashing their heads against the trees. Her father didn't want them to be mistaken for little white children. According to the census records they were called Mulattos. These stories explained why they had such fear of them being mistaken for little white children. After the war between the North and the South, the South would lose the war, and their grip on the Negro slaves.

Another story Grandma Florence often mentioned was Round Lake. It was passed down as oral history, that Round Lake had no bottom and if somene fell into Round Lake, they would never be recovered, because there was no bottom.

Another tale that was passed on about Round Lake was that every seven years a large creature would appear from the lake. Some would say that they had actually seen the creature and that it was larger than a house. As a child, of course, I believed this story. Many of the children of my era, and some of the elders, believed this tale not ever seeing it for ourselves. Looking back, children of my family always loved a good mystery, an old wives' tale, or a story that would stimulate our creativity. Those tales would have a great influence on my life today, some with purpose and others not so uplifting.

My Father's Stories

My father was known for his vivid storytelling. His stories were loved not only by his family but by those outside of the family,

My father often shared ghost stories. We would sit quietly in a circle and listen to stories about a headless horse chasing a woman or a pink rabbit coming into the kitchen. In his story, my dad would grab his rifle and shoot at the rabbit, but it would disappear without being hit. These were the types of stories that he would share on a regular basis. Of course, these are only two among many. Were they true? I don't know. I do know that we loved our dad's storytelling time.

My Mother's Sayings to Live By

Many Black families and indigenous people had lots of sayings and proverbs that they lived by. My foreparents, being of both backgrounds, would pass on many sayings to us. Many of us today still use a lot of these old sayings. They are a part of our culture and make up who we are, as people of indigenous natives, and those ancestors that were brought here to America. Many of our African and indigenous ancestors had the exact same customs and expressions. They would caution their offspring with the same warnings and proverbs either directly from the Bible or with a mixture of their own expressions. Their concern was to make sure that their children got the messages in more ways than one.

In raising my three adult children, I often found myself giving them the same warnings and admonitions. My speeches were always colored with my parents' sayings. Many of these sayings can be deciphered by our grandchildren.

Many were based on scripture, such as "The more things change, the more they remain the same." "There is nothing new under the sun... What has been will be." (The thing that hath been, it is that which shall be; and that which is done is that which shall be done: and there is no new thing under the sun. Ecclesiastes 1:9).

Be not deceived; God is not mocked: for whatsoever a man soweth, that shall he also reap. Galatians 6:7

My mother, Victoria Martha Lamb Carroll, had the oddest sayings. I know not where they originated; however, they would become a part of our lives as we grew up. They were a part of her daily communication to us - in order to get our attention, or to prevent us from heading in the wrong direction - which we often did.

Mother had many sayings and warnings about life. I did not understand many of these warnings at the time and often thought that they made very little sense. Sometimes, I didn't know how to interpret her meaning. However, my five older siblings understood her code messages very well. Now, as I have raised three adult children and experienced a lot in life, I do understand her words of wisdom.

The wisdom of the young - how taxing it can become to parents. When growing up, you feel you know what is best for you, and you want to express yourself and make your own decisions. This is very common among the young. I smile as I recall those words of warnings so many times.

My mother would often say, *"You have the big head"* (You think you know more than you really do). She would also say, *"Don't cut off your nose to spite your face"* (Do not act too quickly, and cause yourself harm).

Another of her favorite sayings was *"Don't take any wooden nickels."* This means do not allow anyone to trick you - do not be deceived with false things, be smart enough to recognize the real from the imposter - do not sell yourself short, below your high standards that you have set for yourself. How many wooden nickels we must have taken as we explored life, searching for so many things that allured us in our searching to live and enjoy life. In life there were beautiful and shining things that would get mama's girls attention. We took more wooden nickels than we should have.

As girls, we were often reminded not to allow the opposite sex to use us. We were instructed daily - do not give yourself away. If my mother suspected you of courting, she would say *"Don't let him get you behind the door or put the big hat on you."* (Don't let him get you pregnant or deceive you).

Mama would always tell us not to get ahead of ourselves. As I pondered this saying many times I recall getting ahead of myself quite frequently, making decisions that I should have paused to give some serious evaluation and advice. However, that was not the case. Instead, I would choose to do things my own way, not heeding any words of wisdom, forgetting to gather all the facts before moving ahead. I have learned that without proper research and wisdom the results more often than not resulted in chaos.

"Getting the Cart Before the Horse" is another old saying or proverb Mama always used. She believed there was a certain order to things and would determine that you were not getting things in the correct order. She was basically correct in most cases. I believe she meant that you should not move ahead without examining every facet of the situation if you wanted to achieve your desired outcome. You needed to be sure every side of the problem was analyzed before moving to the next level for the best possible result. Establish all the known facts about a thing before moving ahead. Not having

basic information about a thing could cause great harm in some instances. Incorporated in this saying is a similar meaning – *"Haste makes waste"* which means don't be anxious about anything. How often was this saying mentioned among the elders of my day.

The scripture for this particular verse says *"Be anxious for nothing but in everything, by prayer and supplication, let your requests be known unto God"* (Philippians 4:6). It is one I've tried to live by.

Mama always reminded us to take our time about things, whether it was making a decision about something, such as a major decision about life, or even an individual. Concerning any matter of life, whether minor or major, we should evaluate the matter very carefully prior to making a final decision. I can remember my mother's warnings about many matters while growing up. She monitored our behavior about a matter, and would determine if we were demonstrating a behavior of being too excited or anxious about moving forward. Many times, even today, I find myself slowing my pace about decision making, checking to make sure, I've not moving too rapidly, resulting in waste.

"Do Not Go Off Half Cocked." My mother would use this phrase to slow us down, or to stop our actions completely. As a young child and even as a teenager, I was often told to slow down before proceeding. As most young teenagers are, I was quite an independent thinker, and quite a reactionary individual. As a result, I would often find my decisions in conflict with her wishes - never operating in all the facts, being half-cocked and moving ahead. As a result, my mother and I did not have the best of relationships but I now understand that it was not her fault, but mainly my own.

Chapter 11

❦

Be Encouraged

"There is now no condemnation for those who walk
after the spirit
and not after the flesh."

Romans 8:1

N o experience or challenge is ever wasted. They are moments that we learn from what we label as mistakes. We take those so-called mistakes and grow from them. We allow them to teach us the lessons that we need to learn and move forward. We are being shaped for the Master's use. We can grow and be a blessing and teach others. We do not need to live in condemnation and feelings of unworthiness. We move forward toward the mark of the higher calling. Jesus reminds us; *"I have come that you may have life and that you may have it more abundantly"* (John 10:10). We forgive ourselves of previously missing the mark in our lives and we *"press toward the prize of the high calling of God in Christ Jesus"* as St. Paul states in Philippians 3:14.

We were made for purpose, and with an assignment. We must find our purpose in life early, and be about the assignment the Creator has given each of us. Many never realize the plan and pur-pose for their lives here. We are only here for a season, and it is important that we find our purpose for our journey here - our journey in this earth realm. We are reminded to seek and find the Creator early. We do not have time to waste.

I must admit that life experiences have shaped me. Life has not left me bitter or without hope - just the contrary. Every challenge, every misstep in life, has shaped me and fashioned me into the individual that I am today. Life's experiences and challenges will shape all of us - some for good and some for not so good. Whatever the case, the Creator desires to shape us for our highest good, and for His Glory.

We all have our challenges and hurdles in life. We must strive to do the same, if we are to find the higher purpose for our life. I have entrusted my life and times in the hands of the Creator. Thus far, His leading, molding and ordering my steps have not failed me. I have grown to understand that there are seasons for everything under the sun (Ecclesiastes 3:1-4).

To everything there is a season, and a time to every pur-pose under the heaven: A time to be born, and a time to die; a time to plant, and a time to pluck up that which is planted; A time to kill, and a time to heal; a time to break down, and a time to build up; A time to weep, and a time to laugh; a time to mourn, and a time to dance;

Giving thanks for these times, the times that we did not understand what life was trying to teach us, the times that we were misunderstood, and the times we were mishandled in life. *"All things, work together for good, to those who love the Lord, and who are the called according to His purpose."* Romans 8:28.

We are being processed for higher works. The Master never left us, not for one moment. His hands were there when we did not realize it. His still, quiet voice was guiding and leading us. He never left us, reminding us that *"...I will never leave you, nor forsake you"* (Hebrews 13:5) but will go with you, all the days of your life, even unto the ends of the earth. We are all vessels on a voyage needing guidance. We are in need of His Spirit to lead us in our daily lives, throughout our time here on this earth. We need His Spirit to shape our destiny, our lying down and our going out.

Arriving at this amazing junction in life truly has been by the grace of a Living God. How grateful I am that He never left me alone. I am aware of my need for His presence and his grace and mercy over my life. Based on the old hymn, "Amazing Grace" he has and is guiding me *"through many dangerous toils and snares..."* . I am assured He will continue to guide me all the days of my life.

The Father knows how much or how little pressure is needed in our lives in order to produce a finished work. We are shaped for the Master's work, realizing moments of closeness, moments of growth, and moments of clarity.

O how I love thee,
O How great is your love toward me.
In times of distress and worry, you've kept me, guided me,
pruned me and kept me close to thee.
O what love and tender mercies I can't explain.
Your power, your grace, your presence,
maketh me realize,
my life, my living has not been in vain.
To God be the Glory, forever and ever.
Amen.

Epilogue

My maternal great-grandparents, Martha and Cornelius Rainey, were gone long before I was born. I long to have known my great grandparents. I can envision the hardships they must have endured – raising fifteen children - their joys, their pain, and their faith in their God. They must have struggled, just as we struggle today, trying to make sense of this life, and how to move forward. Their struggles failed to leave them without hope. They lived lives that would strengthen the generations to come. I can say that I am proud and thankful to have been the results of their struggle.

Truly God has watched over, and has blessed, Cornelius and Martha Rainey. Many of their descendants are still on the earth, trying to fulfill the mission of The Creator in our lives. Hard work and faith has brought us this far. Truly His Grace and His Mercy will carry us on. There have been lots of hurdles, pain, failures, and missing the mark along this journey. However, we will continue to serve the Creator as long as we have our beings. Those of us who are alive today have drawn a line in the sand, and will not turn back. God is worthy of our praise and our thanksgiving. We will pass the legacy on to the coming generations - A legacy that God has kept us, through many dangers, toils and snares and will continue to be with us.

My grandparents demonstrated that they would not cave in to the world they were born into. They were just exiting slavery, being owned by another human being. Now they would be entering a world of Jim Crow laws in America. What decisions were before them? Would they remain on the plantations of their former masters? Would they share crop, or strike out on their own?

Based on oral history, the family would sharecrop. They would prepare for the future as best they could. They were strong people with strong faith and lots of hands to assist in moving the family into the future. Written history as well as oral history, indicated that they lived on the Taylor Plantation. The Rainey's would produce fifteen beautiful, strong offspring.

To our knowledge, Martha and Cornelius never owned their own land. Like many Black families of that era, they lived as sharecroppers for the plantation owners. They were no longer enslaved by chains, but were tied to the land, working the land for a place to get a start, to save money, with the hopes of owning their own land one day. They were enslaved without resources to strike out on their own.

The Rainey's never received their forty aces and a mule - the promise from the government to start their new life of freedom. We, as their descendants, carry that same hope and faith in God and the future, thanking God for their lives that they were able to survive and pass the torch to the next generation. *What giants they were!* They blessed this earth with their presence. *These beautiful people!* I have no pictures of them - only in my mind and word of mouth passed on to me. Observing their names, their ages, and their offspring, and examining these records touched my heart. There were actually records that they lived so long ago. As of this writing, I have found no record of their parents and their foreparents. It would be such a joy to discover who their parents were and how they lived.

We must never forget our ancestors, who were brought to America from Africa. Many were stolen. They would work from sunup to sundown. I now realize that not all Blacks descended from slaves. Many were already here, as natives of the Americas; however, most of our parents were children of slaves. Their bloodshed and their struggles speak to us through the ages. My great grandfather Cornelius's mother (my great-great grandmother) was a slave. She would bear the scars all of her life. She wore a ball and chain around her ankle. This object was used to prevent her constant running off. The indentation around her ankle lasted throughout her life. Her only freedom was found in the grave. May she, along with millions, rest in peace, from their bondage and their endless toil. Amen.

There have been lots of hurdles, pain, failures, and missing the mark along the way. The struggle goes on as long as we are in this earth realm. However, eight of my siblings are still in this earth realm. We still find reason to thank God and to honor Him. We pray that God will give us the strength to finish the work that he has entrusted to each of us and that we may always hear his voice and know His Voice. *To God be the Glory, forever and ever.*

Eternal gratitude and thanksgiving to Cornelius, Martha, Florence, John, Cortez and Victoria Carroll, and John and Rose Carroll. How they stood strong in the midst of struggle and pain. I know they must have had moments of happiness and celebration, along with tears and struggle. We are the proof that their lives were a mixture of both. We are their descendants; our lives are somewhat a reflection of their lives; the blueprint that they left us. We have whole heartily tried to follow it. May they rest in eternal peace.

I thank God for the memories and His leading and guiding me in this project, leaving a written record for those who will come after us. *"To God be all Glory forever and ever."* The ancestors left me courage, a willingness to search out our roots, never giving up, to face challenges with faith and endurance. They left me a mission which I have tried to fulfill - to pass that same guidance and wisdom on to my children.

"May the Lord be gracious unto us, and make His face to shine upon us, for He rules the nations justly. Let the people praise you, Let all the people praise you" *(Psalms 67:1-3 NIV).*

❦❖❦

"LIFT EVERY VOICE AND SING"

Lift every voice and sing
Till earth and heaven ring,
Ring with the harmonies of Liberty;
Let our rejoicing rise
High as the listening skies,
Let it resound loud as the rolling sea.
Sing a song full of the faith that the dark past has taught us,
Sing a song full of the hope that the present has brought us.
Facing the rising sun of our new day begun,
Let us march on till victory is won.
Stony the road we trod,
Bitter the chastening rod,
Felt in the days when hope unborn had died;
Yet with a steady beat,
Have not our weary feet
Come to the place for which our fathers sighed?
We have come over a way that with tears has been watered,
We have come, treading our path through the blood of the slaughtered,
Out from the gloomy past,
Till now we stand at last
Where the white gleam of our bright star is cast.
God of our weary years,
God of our silent tears,
Thou who hast brought us thus far on the way;
Thou who hast by Thy might
Led us into the light,
Keep us forever in the path, we pray.
Lest our feet stray from the places, our God, where we met Thee,
Lest, our hearts drunk with the wine of the world, we forget Thee;
Shadowed beneath Thy hand,
May we forever stand.
True to our God,
True to our native land.

—James Weldon Johnson

Lightning Source UK Ltd.
Milton Keynes UK
UKHW030636140219
337321UK00005B/472/P

9 781545 660089